Praise for *98.6 Mortality Movies to See Before You Die*

"Nothing motivates responsible end-of-life planning like a great movie and the quiet realization that you are not immortal. *98.6 Mortality Movies to See Before You Die* is a great resource for planning your funeral *before* the plot twist, and for pre-need sales professionals, it's an excellent lead generator."

- Rob Meredith, retired Vice President, Precoa

"Movies give people a way to step into conversations about death without being overwhelmed by it. When we create that space – warm, shared, and human – we help families feel less alone and more prepared for whatever comes next. We support Gail and her book in bringing people together for these critical conversations."

- Tom Antram, CEO & Owner, French Funerals & Cremations

"As a lifelong movie fan, I see many of the same themes in *98.6 Mortality Movies to See Before You Die* in the films that I love the most: forgiveness, redemption, and what really matters before the final curtain call. I've spent much of my life telling stories for children, but this book is a wonderful reminder that grown-ups need good stories too. And the best stories remind us of the choices we make and what is really important in the end."

- Barry Louis Polisar, children's author and musician

"Gail Rubin brings clarity, insight, and creativity to one of life's most important conversations. *98.6 Mortality Movies to See Before You Die* shows how film can be a powerful and engaging way to open honest discussions about death, dignity, and choice. Entertaining and thoughtful, this book invites us to reflect on what it means to prepare for a good death and to discuss it more openly with those we love."

– Chris Palmer, author of *Achieving a Good Death:*
A Practical Guide to the End of Life

"What an instant tabletop classic! As someone who loves both movies and meaningful conversations about death, this book is a perfect fit for my Death Café. I've already seen many of the films, and now I've got a checklist for the rest. Pass the popcorn… and the tissues!"

– Diana L. Brooks, Community Engagement Lead,
Foundation Partners Group

"You're not dead yet, but one day you will be. These films will help you prepare with intention instead of fear."

– Kathy Dempsey, RN, MED, CSP, co-author of *You're Not Dead Yet!:*
How to Live Well, Laugh Often and Graduate Life with Honors

"Gail Rubin's latest book, 98.6 Mortality Movies to See Before You Die, is a 'must read' guide for anyone interested in both mortality and film. Whether you are a seasoned deathcare professional, an educator, or a 'death curious' layperson, this book will spark conversations, teachable moments, and countless hours of enjoyable screening time. Supported by the author's passion for film and her extensive work as a Certified Thanatologist and death educator, this book isn't just an enjoyable read – it's a reminder that film is both a reflection of human experience and a way to deepen our understanding of life, love, and mortality."

– Sara E. Murphy, PhD, FT, Death Educator & Suicidologist

98.6
MORTALITY MOVIES
TO SEE BEFORE YOU DIE

REMARKABLE FILMS AND TV SHOWS TO DISCUSS DEATH AND PLAN AHEAD

GAIL RUBIN, CT

Other books by Gail Rubin, CT

A Good Goodbye: Funeral Planning for Those Who Don't Plan to Die

Hail and Farewell: Cremation Ceremonies, Templates and Tips

*Kicking the Bucket List: 100 Downsizing and
Organizing Things to Do Before You Die*

Before I Die Festival in a Box

Dedicated to my late husband David Bleicher,
who shared my passion for film.

"Elevate me."

CONTENTS

INTRODUCTION

Movies are where many of us go to rehearse the big moments of life without leaving our seats: first kisses, last chances, joyful reunions, heartbreaking goodbyes. This book focuses on what I call Mortality Movies: films and television stories that do not merely include a death but engage with what it means to live while knowing life is finite.

These are the stories that help us talk about the one experience we are all guaranteed to share: our deaths.

What Is a Mortality Movie?

A Mortality Movie is not simply any film or television show that includes a funeral. If that were the standard, half of Hollywood would qualify, and this book would be the size of a casket. To earn a place here, a story must meaningfully engage with death, dying, grief, remembrance, or end-of-life planning.

A Mortality Movie might explore how we die, how we mourn, how we remember our dead, or how taking death seriously can change how we live. These stories ask big questions:

What matters?

What lasts?

How do we say goodbye?

How can we plan so our last chapter reflects who we are?

And how can we spare our loved ones from heartbreaking guesswork after we are gone?

You will notice that this book goes beyond traditional feature films. In addition to comedies and dramas, it includes documentaries, animated films, and television programs. Some of the most powerful meditations on mortality appear in television episodes where a single story can open big conversations in under an hour. Carefully chosen episodes are especially useful for classrooms, community programs, and time-limited Mortality Movie Nights.

The films and shows in this book are grouped by theme, including funerals and funeral directors, medical treatment and end-of-life issues, death fantasy and afterlife visions, grief and growth, mortality and living fully, estate planning, and hard-to-categorize Mortality Movies.

What's With the ".6"?

So, what is the ".6" in *98.6 Mortality Movies to See Before You Die*?

There are iconic scenes involving death that do not qualify the entire film as a Mortality Movie yet remain instructive and worth discussing. Think of the ash-scattering scene in *The Big Lebowski*, the cremation chaos in *Meet the Parents*, the funeral in *Four Weddings and a Funeral*, or the historically inaccurate yet wildly influential Viking funeral from *The Vikings*.

These moments matter even if the films themselves do not fully belong in this category.

And while the title promises 98.6, you will find that I exceeded my own assignment. This book includes 142 films and television programs, each with a discussion guide. New films continue to be released. Older ones continue to surface. If I missed your favorite, please accept my apologies and consider this an evolving canon. I will post new film and television program discussion guides at the blog on my website, www.AGoodGoodbye.com.

That said, not every movie with a coffin, cemetery, or graveside monologue makes the cut. In many stories, death is merely a plot device: a convenient way to motivate a hero, trigger a chase scene, or explain why a character is grumpy. This book is not a catalog of cinematic funerals. It is a curated guide to stories that genuinely invite reflection, conversation, and planning.

Mortality Movie Nights

My first Mortality Movie Night took place in 2013 at French Funerals & Cremations, an independent funeral company in Albuquerque, New Mexico. I approached their CEO, Tom Antram, with an idea that was new to funeral home community outreach: Invite people in for a movie rather than a funeral.

We screened two films based on true stories involving funeral directors: *Bernie* and *Get Low*. The events were covered by the local alternative weekly newspaper and quickly proved something important: Watching a movie together creates a safe, welcoming space to talk about mortality.

Mortality Movie Nights allow people to meet funeral home staff outside the stress of a death in the family. They build warm community connections. They open the door to advance planning conversations. One regular attendee eventually prearranged his cremation because of the relationships formed through these gatherings.

In 2025, I revived Mortality Movie Nights with my Death Café community. What started in my living room quickly outgrew the space, leading French Funerals & Cremations to host biweekly screenings in their chapel. They provided the venue and beverages, and I brought the popcorn and chocolate. The conversations that followed were rich, honest, and often surprising.

Legal Considerations

If you have ever watched a DVD or videotape, you have likely seen the ominous warning about unauthorized reproductions or public screenings. While there are no movie police that I know of, it is wise to respect copyright law.

To show films publicly outside a private home, a license is required. For many years, I used an umbrella license from the Motion Picture Licensing Corporation (MPLC). In 2025, they changed their business model, shifting licensing responsibility to venues rather than presenters and restricting promotional use of film titles.

Other companies, including Swank Motion Pictures and Criterion Pictures USA, offer per-event or annual licenses and allow promotion of film titles. Showing films in a private home remains legally protected, which some funeral homes that also function as residences may leverage.

A Passion for Movies and Mortality

I am known as The Doyenne of Death®. As a Certified Thanatologist, I have spent years using humor, films, and community events to get people talking about death long before there is a crisis. In 2024, the Association for Death Education and Counseling honored this work with their Community Educator Award.

My previous books include *A Good Goodbye*, *Kicking the Bucket List*, and *Hail and Farewell*. I was the first person west of the Mississippi River to host a Death Café in 2012 and founded the Before I Die New Mexico Festival in 2017.

Before becoming a death educator, I was a public relations professional with a degree in communications and an emphasis on film and television. I studied classic directors, genres, and film production, including a college project that parodied Ingmar Bergman's *The Seventh Seal* using bubblegum fortunes in place of chess. Death still won.

Over the years, I have watched, rewatched, and discussed these films with funeral professionals, medical teams, faith communities, and everyday people who simply want to be better prepared.

This book is a practical, entertaining guide designed to spark conversation, explore personal beliefs, and encourage thoughtful planning. Whether you are leading a group, teaching a class, or hosting a movie night at home, these stories can help open doors we often keep closed.

Along the way, I had a very modern research assistant: ChatGPT. AI helped organize information and draft discussion guides, which I reviewed, corrected, and confirmed through sources like IMDb. Every film included here is one I have personally seen.

My hope is that *98.6 Mortality Movies to See Before You Die* makes it easier, and even enjoyable, to talk about the things we so often avoid. Watching these stories together, we can laugh, cry, argue, question, and plan.

After all, just as talking about sex won't make you pregnant, talking about funerals won't make you dead. But it just might make life, and the ending of it, a whole lot better.

FUNERALS AND FUNERAL DIRECTORS

Introduction

Funerals sit at the crossroads of grief, ritual, culture, commerce, and love. They are one of the few moments in life where emotion and logistics collide so directly, often at a time when people are least prepared to make decisions. The films in this chapter pull back the curtain on what happens after death, not only to bodies but to families, relationships, and long-held assumptions about how we are "supposed" to say goodbye.

Some of these stories focus on funeral directors themselves, professionals who work daily with death yet must remain deeply human in the face of loss. Others center on families navigating arrangements, misunderstandings, or conflict while trying to honor someone they love. Together, they reveal funerals not as static traditions but as evolving expressions of meaning, values, and connection.

These films remind us that funerals are not really for the dead; they are for the living. They are storytelling events, acts of love, and sometimes sites of healing or reckoning. By watching how others stumble, improvise, and occasionally get it right, we gain permission to imagine what a meaningful farewell might look like for ourselves and those we care about.

Bernie *(2011, PG-13, 1 h 44 min)*

Starring: Jack Black, Shirley MacLaine, Matthew McConaughey

Directed by: Richard Linklater

Film Description

Based on a true story, *Bernie* follows Bernie Tiede, a relentlessly kind church-going assistant funeral director in the small town of Carthage, Texas. Bernie befriends Marjorie Nugent, a wealthy widow known for her sharp tongue and impossible demands. As her emotional and financial dependence on him escalates, Bernie commits a shocking crime: He murders Marjorie and hides her body in a freezer. For months afterward, he maintains the illusion that she is still alive but ill, all while using her money to support local charities, schools, and neighbors.

What makes *Bernie* so unsettling is not just the crime but the community's reaction. Many townspeople defend Bernie, crediting him with generosity, compassion, and moral goodness. The film offers a darkly comic and surprisingly thoughtful look at the funeral profession, small-town dynamics, moral blind spots, and what happens when caretaking boundaries disappear.

Mortality Themes

- The emotional labor of funeral directors and caretakers
- Boundary erosion in grief work and caregiving roles
- Power, dependency, and control in relationships involving the vulnerable
- Community complicity and moral rationalization
- Overlap between death work and money, trust, and authority

Discussion Prompts

1. Bernie is widely loved by the community, even after his crime is revealed. Why do people excuse or minimize his actions?

2. How does Bernie's role as a funeral director shape the trust others place in him?

3. Where should professional boundaries exist in caregiving and death-related work? What happens when they blur?

4. The townspeople benefit financially from Bernie's actions. How does this complicate their moral judgment?

5. What does the film suggest about loneliness, control, and emotional dependency in later life?

6. How does humor function in this film? Does it make the story easier or harder to confront?

Movie Pairings and Activities

- Pair the movie with *Sunshine Cleaning* (2008) for a very different look at death work, professionalism, and personal boundaries.

- Or pair it with *The Funeral* (1996) to compare how communities respond to death, crime, and loyalty.

- Discuss ethical boundaries in caregiving roles. Where does kindness end and responsibility begin? Consider parallels in hospice care, elder care, and funeral service.

Final Thought

Bernie reminds us that even the gentlest professions require firm boundaries. Compassion without limits can quietly turn into control, and good intentions are not the same as ethical behavior. In the world of funerals and funeral directors, trust is essential, but so is accountability. This film challenges us to look beyond charm and ask harder questions about power, responsibility, and the quiet dangers of being "too nice" in the presence of grief.

Death at a Funeral *(2007, R, 1 h 30 min | 2010, R, 1 h 32 min)*

Starring:

- *2007 (UK version):* Matthew Macfadyen, Alan Tudyk, Keeley Hawes, Peter Dinklage

- *2010 (US version):* Chris Rock, Martin Lawrence, Zoe Saldaña, Peter Dinklage

Directed by: Frank Oz (both versions)

Film Description

This farce-filled comedy unfolds almost entirely during the funeral of a family patriarch, where grief, resentment, secrets, and pharmaceuticals collide. As relatives gather at the family home for the service, everything that can go wrong does. The arrival of a mysterious stranger who threatens to expose a scandal involving the deceased sends the already fragile family dynamic into a full meltdown.

Both versions follow the same basic structure, with cultural nuances shaping the humor. The British original leans dry and restrained, while the American remake is louder and broader, but each highlights how funerals can amplify long-simmering family tensions. The home funeral setting adds intimacy and pressure, turning the service into a crucible for truth, embarrassment, and unintended confession.

Mortality Themes

- Funerals as emotional pressure cookers for families
- Home funerals and their logistical and emotional challenges
- Financial stress surrounding funeral costs
- The weight of secrets carried beyond death
- The gap between public remembrance and private truth

Discussion Prompts

1. Why do funerals so often become flashpoints for unresolved family conflict?

2. How does holding the funeral at home change the emotional intensity of the event?

3. What obligations, if any, do families have to protect a deceased person's reputation?

4. How do cultural expectations shape how grief and decorum are expressed at funerals?

5. What does the film suggest about the pressure to present a "perfect" funeral experience?

6. If this funeral had gone "according to plan," what important truths would have remained hidden, and would that have been better or worse for the family?

Movie Pairings and Activities

- Pair the movie with *Bernie* (2011) to explore how death exposes community and family blind spots.

- Or pair it with *The Big Chill* (1983) for another look at how death reunites people who would rather not be together.

- Ask participants to list what makes a funeral feel meaningful versus performative. Where does honesty fit into remembrance?

Final Thought

Death at a Funeral reminds us that, while death is universal, mourning is deeply personal and often messy. Funerals are rarely just about the person who died. They are about the living, their unfinished business, and their imperfect attempts to honor a life while holding themselves together. If nothing else, the film reassures us that, if your family funeral feels chaotic, awkward, or emotionally charged, you are in very good company.

The Death of Stalin *(2017, R, 1 h 47 min)*

Starring: Steve Buscemi, Simon Russell Beale, Jason Isaacs, Michael Palin

Directed by: Armando Iannucci

Film Description

When Soviet dictator Joseph Stalin suddenly collapses and dies in 1953, the power vacuum he leaves behind is instant, vicious, and absurd. As members of the council of ministers scramble to secure influence, rewrite history, and avoid becoming the next political casualty, the logistics of Stalin's funeral become just another battlefield. Who speaks? Who stands closest to the coffin? Who survives the week?

This razor-sharp political satire treats death not as a moment of reverence but as a strategic opportunity. Funeral planning becomes an extension of governance, propaganda, and fear management, revealing how rituals meant to honor the dead can be co-opted to serve the living. The film is profane, fast talking, and relentless, but beneath the comedy lies a chilling truth about power and mortality.

Mortality Themes

- Death as a political event rather than a personal loss
- Funerals as tools for legacy control and public messaging
- Who gets to speak for the dead and who gets silenced
- The contrast between public mourning and private relief
- The fragility of authority once a powerful figure dies

Discussion Prompts

1. How does the film portray the difference between public grief and private reaction?
2. In what ways is Stalin's funeral more about the future than the past?
3. Who controls legacy after death, and how is that power negotiated or fought over?

4. How do funerals for public figures differ from those of private individuals?

5. What does the film suggest about fear, loyalty, and honesty in the face of death?

6. What parts of the funeral felt genuinely ritualistic, and which felt purely performative or strategic? How could you tell the difference?

Movie Pairings and Activities

- Pair the movie with *Bernie* (2011) to compare how death affects small-town power versus national power.

- Or pair it with *The Queen* (2006) to examine how public mourning is shaped by political necessity.

- Ask participants to reflect on high-profile funerals they remember. What messages were being sent, and by whom?

Final Thought

The Death of Stalin strips the sentimentality out of death and replaces it with naked ambition. It reminds us that funerals do not exist in a vacuum. They are shaped by culture, hierarchy, and the needs of those still breathing. While most of us will never plan a dictator's funeral, the film offers a darkly funny lesson on how death reveals the truth about power, priorities, and the stories people rush to tell when a voice can no longer contradict them.

Departures *(2008, PG-13, 2 h 10 min)*

Starring: Masahiro Motoki, Ryōko Hirosue, Tsutomu Yamazaki

Directed by: Yōjirō Takita

Film Description

In this Oscar-winning Japanese drama, Daigo Kobayashi is an unemployed cellist who reluctantly accepts a job he initially misunderstands. He soon discovers he has become a *nōkanshi*, a professional who prepares the dead for burial through a meticulous and ritualized ceremony performed in front of grieving families. Ashamed of the work at first, Daigo slowly comes to understand the dignity, intimacy, and emotional power of caring for the dead.

As Daigo learns the craft, the film gently reveals how death touches every part of life, including marriage, friendship, and unresolved family wounds. *Departures* offers a rare, reverent look at funeral work not as something morbid but as an act of service, artistry, and compassion.

Mortality Themes

- Encountering death as a meaningful human experience
- Funeral rituals as bridges between the living and the deceased
- Cultural traditions surrounding death, cremation, and mourning
- Grief that is hidden, delayed, or quietly carried
- Finding purpose and dignity in death-care work

Discussion Prompts

1. How does the film change your perception of people who work with the dead?
2. Why do you think Daigo initially feels shame about his job, and how does that shift?
3. What role does ritual play in helping families say goodbye?
4. How does the film portray grief differently across characters and generations?
5. What cultural differences stood out to you in how death and funerals are handled?
6. How does witnessing the preparation of the body change the way the characters, and possibly viewers, relate to death itself?

Movie Pairings and Activities

- Pair the movie with *Six Feet Under* (TV series) to compare Western and Japanese approaches to death care.
- Or pair it with *Wit* (2001) to explore dignity at the end of life from different perspectives.
- Invite viewers to reflect on a funeral or memorial they found especially meaningful. What elements made it so?

Final Thought

Departures is a quiet, beautiful reminder that caring for the dead is not about morbidity but about love, respect, and closure. It suggests that, when we treat the final acts of life with intention and grace, we also heal the living. This film often leaves audiences more open, more tender, and perhaps a little less afraid of the work that happens after death.

Elizabethtown *(2005, PG-13, 2 h 3 min)*

Starring: Orlando Bloom, Kirsten Dunst, Susan Sarandon

Directed by: Cameron Crowe

Film Description

This romantic comedy with a wonderful soundtrack unfolds in the wake of multiple life disruptions. Drew Baylor is reeling from professional failure and deep depression when his father dies suddenly. He travels from Oregon to Elizabethtown, Kentucky, to attend the funeral and help his exuberant Southern relatives plan an elaborate memorial. Along the way, he meets Claire, a quirky flight attendant who gently guides him through grief, reflection, and the possibility of starting over.

The film draws playful and poignant parallels between weddings and funerals as communal rituals while also highlighting the regional differences in attitudes toward burial, cremation, and remembrance. An over-the-top memorial service and a carefully planned ash-scattering road trip become catalysts for healing, self-discovery, and reconnection.

Mortality Themes

- Funerals and weddings as parallel life rituals
- Cultural differences around burial, cremation, and mourning
- Complicated grief following sudden death
- Memory, legacy, and storytelling as healing tools
- Renewal and second chances after loss

Discussion Prompts

1. How does the film compare weddings and funerals as community events?

2. What cultural contrasts around death and funerals stood out to you?

3. How does Drew's grief differ from that of his extended family?

4. What role does music play in processing loss and memory in the film?

5. How does the ash-scattering journey function as both ritual and therapy?

6. What does the film suggest about who gets to design remembrance rituals, the grieving individual or the wider family or community?

Movie Pairings and Activities

- Pair the movie with *Garden State* (2004) for another story of grief, travel, and emotional awakening.

- Or pair it with *Big Fish* (2003) to explore storytelling as a legacy.

- Invite participants to design their own meaningful memorial ritual, traditional or unconventional.

Final Thought

Elizabethtown suggests that grief does not always arrive quietly or solemnly. Sometimes it shows up with casseroles, eccentric relatives, loud music, and unexpected kindness. The film reminds us that remembrance does not have to be somber to be sincere and that healing often happens when we allow ourselves to be carried forward by connection, humor, and the open road. In its warm, wandering way, the film shows that the voyage through loss may be messy and meandering, but it's also where we rediscover connection, meaning, and the courage to keep going.

Eulogy *(2004, R, 1 h 31 min)*

Starring: Zooey Deschanel, Hank Azaria, Ray Romano, Kelly Preston, Rip Torn

Directed by: Jesse Peretz

Film Description

This sharp-edged black comedy begins, appropriately enough, with a funeral that goes sideways fast. When the blunt and famously unkind patriarch of the Collins family dies, three generations gather to lay him to rest. What follows is a cascade of revelations, resentments, and long-buried family secrets that spill out almost as freely as the wine.

As relatives struggle to craft a respectful eulogy for a man few actually liked, the film skewers the emotional minefield of funerals: unresolved relationships, inheritance tensions, awkward rituals, and the pressure to say something meaningful when the truth is complicated. Along the way, it also delivers some surprisingly instructive (and absurd) moments around unconventional funeral ideas, including a do-it-yourself Viking-style sendoff.

Mortality Themes

- The difficulty of writing an honest eulogy
- Family secrets revealed after death
- Estate planning and inheritance tensions
- Humor as a coping mechanism in grief
- The gap between public remembrance and private truth

Discussion Prompts

1. Is it possible, or even necessary, to speak kindly of someone who caused pain in life?
2. What responsibilities do we have when delivering a eulogy: honesty, compassion, restraint, or performance?
3. How does unresolved family conflict complicate grief after death?
4. What does the film suggest about planning funerals in advance versus leaving decisions to survivors?

5. Where is the line between meaningful ritual and spectacle when it comes to funerals?

6. How might this funeral have been different if the deceased had left clear guidance about how he wanted to be remembered, of if he had addressed conflicts while alive?

Movie Pairings and Activities

- Pair the movie with *Death at a Funeral* (2007) for another chaotic, secret-filled funeral comedy.

- Or pair it with *Bernie* (2011) to examine public perception versus private reality after death.

- Invite participants to draft two versions of a eulogy: one polite and public, one honest and private.

Final Thought

Eulogy reminds us that death does not magically resolve unfinished business. Funerals can be as messy, funny, and uncomfortable as the families who attend them. By leaning into dark humor, the film makes a pointed observation: Planning ahead, telling the truth while we're alive, and addressing family dynamics early might spare our loved ones from having to improvise meaning at the podium later.

The Farewell *(2019, PG, 1 h 40 min)*

Starring: Awkwafina, Zhao Shuzhen, Tzi Ma

Directed by: Lulu Wang

Film Description

When a Chinese family learns that their beloved grandmother has terminal cancer, they make a collective decision not to tell her. Instead, they plan a lavish wedding as a pretext to gather everyone together for what may be their final goodbye. Based on director Lulu Wang's own family experience, *The Farewell* quietly unfolds around shared meals, withheld truths, and the tension between love and honesty.

Mortality Themes

- Anticipatory grief
- Cultural differences in truth-telling and medical disclosure
- Collective versus individual approaches to dying
- Ritual as a container for unspoken goodbyes
- Living fully while death is approaching

Discussion Prompts

1. Who does the truth belong to at the end of life: the patient or the family?
2. How do cultural values shape what we consider "a good death"?
3. Is withholding medical information an act of protection, love, or denial?
4. What rituals in the film function as goodbyes without explicitly saying goodbye?
5. How does anticipatory grief show up differently than grief after death?
6. If you were in this family, what would feel most compassionate to you and why?

Movie Pairings and Activities

- Pair the movie with *Wit* (2001) or *Still Alice* (2014) to compare Western and Eastern approaches to prognosis disclosure.
- Invite viewers to reflect on how their own families handle difficult truths.
- Use the film as a starting point to discuss advance care planning and who should receive medical information.

Final Thought

The Farewell reminds us that love does not always speak plainly. Sometimes it cooks, gathers, celebrates, and holds silence. In this story, grief begins before death arrives, carried quietly in the spaces between words and shared not through explanation but through presence. It's a poignant reminder to savor connection, embrace ritual, and maybe call your grandma.

Get Low *(2009, PG-13, 1 h 43 min)*

Starring: Robert Duvall, Bill Murray, Sissy Spacek

Directed by: Aaron Schneider

Based on: The true story of Felix "Bush" Breazeale

Film Description

Set in rural Tennessee during the 1930s, *Get Low* tells the story of Felix Bush, a lifelong recluse who shocks his small town by announcing he wants to throw his own funeral while he's still alive. He places a newspaper ad inviting anyone with a grievance, a memory, or a bone to pick to attend. What follows is part funeral planning, part confession, and part reckoning.

As Bush works with a local undertaker to organize the event, the film offers a thoughtful look at the evolution of the funeral business and the practical realities of planning a service that breaks every social rule. Beneath the novelty, the story slowly reveals a man burdened by guilt, grief, and isolation, seeking absolution before it's too late.

Mortality Themes

- Living funerals and pre-need planning
- Legacy, regret, and public confession
- Community memory and collective storytelling
- The role of funeral directors as facilitators, not just service providers
- Ritual as a pathway to truth and reconciliation

Discussion Prompts

1. What motivates Felix Bush to hold his funeral while alive: control, confession, forgiveness, or something else?

2. How does a "living funeral" change the purpose of a memorial service?

3.   What role does the undertaker play beyond logistics in this story?

4.   How does community participation shape the meaning of ritual and remembrance?

5.   What conversations might be easier to have while someone is still living rather than after death?

6.   What risks and benefits come with giving people the chance to speak openly to the person being remembered rather than about them afterward?

Movie Pairings and Activities

- Pair the movie with *Elizabethtown* (2005) for unconventional memorials and road-trip remembrance.

- Or pair it with *The Last Word* (2017) for another take on shaping one's legacy in advance.

- Ask viewers to imagine their own "living eulogy." What would they want said, and what would they want to change before it's true?

Final Thought

Get Low gently reminds us that funerals are not just about death; they are about truth, accountability, and the stories we leave behind. By flipping the script and letting the guest of honor listen in, the film makes a compelling case for addressing unfinished business while we still have a voice. After all, the best time to shape your legacy is before someone else has to guess at it.

Getting Grace *(2017, PG-13, 1 h 52 min)*

Starring: Mena Suvari, Daniel Roebuck, Madeline Carroll

Directed by: Daniel Roebuck

Film Description

Getting Grace centers on Grace, a bright, curious, and terminally ill teenager who refuses to let her diagnosis define her spirit. Instead of retreating into despair, she does something unexpected: She walks into a funeral home and starts asking questions, lots of them.

Her frank curiosity about death, funerals, and what happens afterward disrupts the quiet routines of a reserved funeral director and gently transforms everyone she encounters. Through humor, honesty, and awkwardly wonderful conversations, the film offers an unusually tender look at how funeral professionals, families, and even strangers can connect through openness rather than fear.

Mortality Themes

- Teen illness and confronting mortality at a young age
- Curiosity about death as a healthy response
- Funeral homes as places of education, care, and humanity
- Intergenerational connection around end-of-life conversations
- Finding meaning and joy even while dying

Discussion Prompts

1. How does Grace's openness about death change the way others respond to her?
2. What makes her approach to dying feel refreshing rather than tragic?
3. How does the funeral director's role expand beyond professional boundaries?
4. What questions about death do we avoid that Grace asks without hesitation?
5. How might earlier conversations about death reduce fear and misunderstanding?
6. How might funeral homes, families or communities change if curiosity about death were welcomed rather than avoided, especially among children and teens?

Movie Pairings and Activities

- Pair the movie with *Departures* (2008) for a compassionate look at funeral professionals.
- Or pair it with *The Fault in Our Stars* (2014) to compare teen perspectives on mortality.

- Invite participants to write down one question about death they've always wondered about but never asked, then discuss how curiosity can be a form of courage.

Final Thought

Getting Grace reminds us that talking about death doesn't make life smaller. It makes it richer, braver, and more honest. Grace's gift isn't her acceptance of dying but her insistence on understanding it. In doing so, she models something funeral directors know well: When we meet death with curiosity instead of fear, meaningful conversations can begin.

Grand Theft Parsons *(2003, PG-13, 1 h 28 min)*

Starring: Johnny Knoxville, Robert Forster, Christina Applegate

Directed by: David Caffrey

Film Description

Based on a stranger-than-fiction true story, *Grand Theft Parsons* recounts what happened after musician Gram Parsons died of an overdose in 1973 at age twenty-six. His road manager and friend Phil Kaufman steals Parsons' body from Los Angeles International Airport to honor a verbal pact they made to "set his spirit free" in the California desert at Joshua Tree. What follows is a ramshackle road trip involving hearses, mortuary paperwork, and one deeply unconventional attempt at body disposition.

Mortality Themes

- Honoring final wishes, written or not
- The legal versus emotional ownership of a body
- Friendship and loyalty after death
- The chaos that follows when plans are unclear
- The legality of handwritten holographic wills

Discussion Prompts

1. What happens when final wishes are not documented in a will or advance directive?

2. Who has the legal authority to decide what happens to a body after death, and how does that differ from emotional authority?

3. Is fulfilling a personal promise ever more important than following the law?

4. How does this film challenge traditional ideas of what counts as a "respectful" disposition?

5. What planning steps could have prevented the chaos that follows Gram Parsons' death?

6. What does this story reveal about the difference between being remembered accurately versus being remembered romantically or mythically?

Movie Pairings and Activities

- Pair the movie with *Elizabethtown* (2005) or *Bonneville* (2006) to explore ash scattering and road-trip mourning.

- Use it as a case study for discussing the importance of written instructions and designated agents.

- Invite viewers to reflect on how they would want their wishes honored and by whom.

Final Thought

Grand Theft Parsons is funny, messy, and oddly tender. Beneath the absurdity lies a serious lesson: When wishes live only in conversation and not on paper, grief can turn into confusion, conflict, and chaos. Sometimes love drives people to extraordinary acts. Sometimes it just drives a stolen hearse into the desert.

Happy Funeral *(2008, Unrated, 1 h 40 min)*

Starring: Woon-Ling Hau, Eric Tsang, Him Law

Directed by: Barbara Wong Chun-Chun

Film Description

In this Chinese-language film (with English subtitles), a group of young people struggle make a living with their varied interests in movies, music, and writing. After visiting the funeral of a friend's grandmother with strict mourning traditions, they hit on the idea of creating "Happy Funerals." They approach a traditional funeral director who secretly admires their creativity. He asks them for a proposal on how this would make money. They fall short describing the business side of funerals. Instead, they show him an example of what they have in mind, and it's not well received.

When their beloved landlady dies, the group creates a personalized, meaningful, and joy-filled send-off that celebrates her individuality: vibrant music, heartfelt storytelling, new rituals based on their relationships, and multimedia tributes. The traditional funeral director experiences their Happy Funeral, leaving impressed and hopeful for new approaches to personalizing send-offs.

Mortality Themes

- Cultural traditions versus evolving funeral practices
- Personalization of funeral rituals
- Generational differences in how grief is expressed
- The role of joy, humor, and meaning in remembrance
- Respecting the dead by honoring who they really were

Discussion Prompts

1. What makes a funeral "appropriate," and who gets to decide that?
2. How do cultural traditions support people in grief, and when might they feel limiting?
3. Can joy, humor, and celebration coexist with mourning without diminishing respect?

4.   How do generational differences shape expectations around funeral rituals?

5.   What elements of the "Happy Funeral" felt most meaningful and why?

6.   How might funeral professionals balance cultural tradition with innovation while still maintaining trust and credibility within their communities?

Movie Pairings and Activities

- Pair the movie with *Departures* (2008) to compare Eastern funeral traditions and professional roles.

- Or pair it with *Elizabethtown* (2005) or *Get Low* (2009) to discuss personalization and nontraditional services.

- Invite viewers to imagine what elements would make a funeral feel meaningful for them or a loved one.

Final Thought

Happy Funeral reminds us that honoring the dead does not require solemnity alone. Sometimes respect looks like laughter, music, color, and creativity. When the ritual reflects the life that was lived, funerals can become not just endings but affirmations of connection, memory, and love.

Harold and Maude *(1971, PG-13, 1 h 31 min)*

Starring: Ruth Gordon, Bud Cort

Directed by: Hal Ashby

Film Description

This cult classic pairs Harold, a wealthy and deeply alienated young man obsessed with death, with Maude, a spirited woman in her late seventies who delights in life's absurdities. The two meet at funerals, which Harold attends recreationally and Maude treats as social opportunities. Their unlikely friendship evolves into a transformative relationship as Maude challenges Harold's morbid fixation and introduces him to curiosity, rebellion, and joy.

The film is underscored by a memorable Cat Stevens soundtrack, perfectly capturing its blend of melancholy and exuberance.

Mortality Themes

- Obsession with death versus engagement with life
- Funerals as social rituals and meeting places
- Generational wisdom and mentorship
- Autonomy, choice, and exiting life on one's own terms
- Finding meaning through connection and play

Discussion Prompts

1. Why do funerals draw both Harold and Maude, and for very different reasons?
2. How does Maude model a relationship with death that supports living fully?
3. Where is the line between romanticizing death and confronting it honestly?
4. How does the film challenge conventional ideas about age, purpose, and timing in life?
5. What moments in the film most clearly illustrate death as a lens for living?
6. How does Maude's approach to death challenge the idea that acceptance of mortality must look solemn or restrained?

Movie Pairings and Activities

- Pair the movie with *Get Low* (2009) to discuss self-authored rituals and legacy.
- Or pair it with *The Seventh Seal* (1957) for contrasting tones in philosophical engagement with death.
- Invite viewers to reflect on who has helped them shift their perspective on life and mortality.

Final Thought

Harold and Maude doesn't treat death as something to fear or avoid but as a powerful lens that clarifies how precious life really is. Its enduring charm lies in its radical suggestion that embracing mortality may be the very thing that teaches us how to live.

Just Buried *(2007, PG-13, 1 h 34 min)*

Starring: Jay Baruchel, Rose Byrne

Directed by: Chaz Thorne

Film Description

In this offbeat romantic comedy, Oliver Whittaker, a struggling young man, inherits a nearly bankrupt funeral home from his estranged father. He arrives in a small town where business is slow because, inconveniently, hardly anyone is dying. As Oliver learns the ropes of funeral service, he falls for the smart, capable female mortician already on staff. Along the way, the film offers surprisingly detailed explanations of embalming, illustrates the hazards of cremation when pacemakers are overlooked, and explores the nuts and bolts of keeping a funeral home afloat.

Mortality Themes

- The funeral home as both business and community service
- Professional care of the dead and technical realities of death work
- Legacy and inheritance, financial and emotional
- Finding purpose in unexpected places
- Love and growth amid mortality

Discussion Prompts

1. How does the film balance humor with respect for death-care work?
2. What misconceptions about funeral homes does it reinforce or dispel?
3. How does inheriting the funeral home shape Oliver's understanding of his father?

4. What does the film suggest about the sustainability of death care as a business?

5. In what ways does working with the dead help Oliver grow personally?

6. What ethical responsibilities do funeral professionals have when financial survival conflicts with serving families honestly and compassionately?

Movie Pairings and Activities

- Pair the movie with *Six Feet Under* (TV series 2001-2005) for a more dramatic look at running a funeral home.

- Or pair it with *Bernie* (2011) to compare very different portrayals of funeral directors.

- Use the movie as a springboard to discuss what really happens behind the scenes in funeral service.

Final Thought

Just Buried may play death for laughs, but it sneaks in a surprising amount of real-world education about funeral practices. Beneath the quirkiness is a reminder that caring for the dead is meaningful work, even when business is slow, and love shows up in unexpected places.

Last Flag Flying *(2017, R, 2 h 5 min)*

Starring: Steve Carell, Bryan Cranston, Laurence Fishburne

Directed by: Richard Linklater

Film Description

Thirty years after serving together in Vietnam, former Navy Corpsman Larry "Doc" Shepherd reunites with his old Marine buddies Sal Nealon and Richard Mueller for a mission none of them wanted: burying Doc's son, a young Marine killed in the Iraq War. What begins as a straightforward military burial becomes a road trip marked by memories, buried truths, gallows humor, and moral reckoning. The film blends comedy and quiet sorrow as these men navigate grief, friendship, and the meaning of service.

Mortality Themes

- Parental grief and the loss of a child
- Military death and ritualized mourning
- Honoring the dead versus questioning the narrative around war
- Friendship as a lifeline in grief
- Truth-telling, legacy, and moral injury

Discussion Prompts

1. How do military funerals shape the way grief is expressed or constrained?

2. What role does humor play for these men as they confront loss and trauma?

3. How does the film explore the tension between official honors and personal truth?

4. In what ways does shared history help or complicate their grieving process?

5. How does the journey itself function as a form of ritual and mourning?

6. How does the film ask viewers to distinguish between honoring sacrifice and questioning the systems that led to the loss?

Movie Pairings and Activities

- Pair the movie with *Taking Chance* (2009) for another portrayal of military death and honor.
- Or pair it with *Brian's Song* (1971) to explore male friendship and loss across different contexts.
- Use the movie as a discussion starter on how rituals can both comfort and obscure painful realities.

Final Thought

Last Flag Flying reminds us that funerals do more than honor the dead. They reopen old wounds, bring to surface unfinished conversations, and sometimes force the living to confront truths they have avoided for decades. In the end, the film suggests that showing up for one another may be the most meaningful salute of all.

The Loved One *(1965, Unrated, 2 h 2 min)*

Starring: Robert Morse, Jonathan Winters, Rod Steiger, Anjanette Comer, Liberace

Directed by: Tony Richardson

Film Description

This jet-black satire takes aim squarely at the American funeral industry, Hollywood style. A young British poet named Dennis Barlow travels to Los Angeles and moves in with his uncle. After his uncle's unexpected death, Barlow is tasked with arranging his uncle's funeral. He stumbles into a surreal world of salesmanship, status, and spectacle surrounding death. He enters the world of Whispering Glades, a glossy cemetery and mortuary where grief is carefully packaged and aggressively upsold. From casket showrooms to embalming care centers to pet funerals, nothing is spared. Liberace's cameo as an outrageously flamboyant casket salesman is worth the price of admission alone.

Mortality Themes

- Commercialization of death and funerals
- Consumerism versus authenticity in mourning
- Satire as a social critique of death denial
- The discomfort Americans have with mortality
- The absurdity that can arise when grief meets salesmanship

Discussion Prompts

1. What parts of the funeral industry does the film exaggerate, and what still feels uncomfortably accurate?
2. How does humor make it easier or harder to critique sensitive topics like death and grief?

3. Where is the line between honoring the dead and exploiting the living?

4. What does the film suggest about Americans' discomfort with mortality?

5. Does satire help us talk more honestly about death, or does it allow us to keep it at arm's length?

6. How might a family balance transparency about costs and options with the desire to create a meaningful, emotionally resonant service?

Movie Pairings and Activities

- Pair the movie with *Bernie* (2011) for a darker, modern look at funeral professionals and community perception.

- Or pair it with *Six Feet Under* (TV series 2001-2005) to contrast satire with a more intimate portrayal of funeral work.

- Use the movie as a springboard for discussing consumer rights, the Funeral Rule, and personalization in funerals today.

Final Thought

The Loved One dares to say the quiet part out loud: When death becomes a product, grief can become a transaction. By pushing everything to absurd extremes, the film exposes real discomforts that still linger around funerals, money, and meaning. It's outrageous, unsettling, and often hilarious, reminding us that laughter can sometimes be the sharpest tool for examining how we care for the dead and the living alike.

My Girl *(1991, PG, 1 h 42 min)*

Starring: Anna Chlumsky, Macaulay Culkin, Dan Aykroyd, Jamie Lee Curtis

Directed by: Howard Zieff

Film Description

Set in the early 1970s, *My Girl* tells the coming-of-age story of eleven-year-old Vada Sultenfuss, a bright, anxious child growing up in a small Pennsylvania town where her father owns and operates the local funeral home. Vada's mother died giving birth to her, a loss that quietly shapes her fears, curiosity, and worldview. As she navigates friendships, first love, and the confusion of growing up, death is simply part of the landscape of her everyday life. The funeral home is not eerie or grotesque but familiar, human, and oddly comforting.

Mortality Themes

- Childhood encounters with death and grief
- Growing up in a funeral home environment
- Parental loss and unresolved mourning
- Funeral directors as whole people, not just professionals
- How early experiences with death shape anxiety, curiosity, and compassion

Discussion Prompts

1. How does growing up around death affect Vada's understanding of life and loss?
2. What does the film show about the emotional lives of funeral directors and their families?
3. How is childhood grief portrayed differently from adult grief?
4. In what ways does the film normalize death without minimizing its impact?
5. How might early, honest exposure to death shape empathy and resilience later in life?
6. How can adults create spaces where children feel safe asking questions about death without overwhelming them?

Movie Pairings and Activities

- Pair the movie with *Departures* (2008) to compare cultural approaches to working with the dead.
- Or pair it with *Six Feet Under* (TV series 2001-2005) to explore family life inside funeral homes across generations.

- Use the movie as a conversation starter about talking with children honestly and gently about death.

Final Thought

My Girl reminds us that death does not have to be hidden from children to protect them. Instead, when handled with honesty and care, it can become part of a meaningful understanding of life, love, and loss. Tender, funny, and heartbreaking in equal measure, the film shows that growing up around death can foster empathy, resilience, and a deep appreciation for the fragility of being human.

My Mexican Shivah *(2007, Not Rated, 1 h 38 min)*

Starring: David Ostrosky, Raquel Pankowsky, Sergio Kleiner

Directed by: Alejandro Springall

Film Description

This Mexican comedy centers on a Jewish family in Mexico City as they navigate the death of a loved one and observe traditional Jewish mourning practices. The story moves from the rituals surrounding death and burial into the seven-day mourning period known as shivah. Language, personalities, old grievances, and cultural misunderstandings all collide as family members gather under one roof. The result is a heartfelt, often funny portrayal of grief shaped by ritual, memory, and community. Dialogue is in Spanish and Yiddish with English subtitles.

Mortality Themes

- Jewish funeral and mourning traditions
- Ritual as structure for grief
- Cultural identity and intergenerational tension
- Community support during mourning
- Humor as a companion to sorrow

Discussion Prompts

1. How do ritual and structure help people navigate grief?
2. What role does community play during extended mourning periods like shivah?
3. How does humor function within sacred or solemn traditions?
4. In what ways does culture shape how grief is expressed or restrained?
5. What elements of shivah might be helpful outside a religious context?
6. What happens when personal grief does not align neatly with pre-scribed ritual timelines or expectations?

Movie Pairings and Activities

- Pair the movie with *The Farewell* (2019) to compare cultural approaches to mourning and truth-telling.
- Or pair it with *Nora's Will* (2008) to more deeply explore Jewish funeral traditions.
- Invite viewers to share or research mourning rituals from their own cultural or religious backgrounds.

Final Thought

My Mexican Shivah gently demonstrates that grief is never just private. It unfolds in kitchens, living rooms, shared meals, and awkward conversations. Through ritual, laughter, and collective presence, the film shows how mourning traditions offer not only comfort for the dead but a roadmap for the living as they stumble their way back toward balance.

Nora's Will *(2008, Not Rated, 1 h 32 min)*

Starring: Fernando Luján, Enrique Arreola, Ari Brickman

Directed by: Mariana Chenillo

Film Description

This award-winning Mexican comedy drama begins with a shock: Nora dies by suicide just before Passover and Shabbat. Her ex-husband José is suddenly pulled back into her life, tasked with managing the practical, religious, and emotional consequences of her death. As José struggles to coordinate Jewish funeral customs, holiday observances, and family tensions, he uncovers carefully orchestrated choices Nora made before she died. The film unfolds with warmth, restraint, and surprising humor, revealing how grief and reconciliation can coexist in unexpected ways. Dialogue is in Spanish with English subtitles.

Mortality Themes

- Jewish funeral and mourning practices
- Suicide and its impact on loved ones
- Ritual obligations versus emotional readiness
- Presence with the dead before burial
- Timing, holidays, and the logistics of death
- Grief as a path toward understanding and forgiveness

Discussion Prompts

1. How do religious traditions shape responses to suicide, and how have those responses evolved?
2. What role do rituals play when emotions are unresolved or complicated?
3. How does caring for the dead affect the emotional journey of the living?
4. Can intention and preparation soften the chaos that often follows death?
5. How do timing and circumstances, such as holidays, location, and relationships, shape grief?
6. How does caring for Nora's body and honoring ritual obligations reshape José's understanding of their relationship?

Movie Pairings and Activities

- Pair the movie with *My Mexican Shivah* (2007) to explore traditional Jewish mourning traditions in contemporary Mexico.

- Or pair it with *The Farewell* (2019) to discuss the cultural expectations around death and truth.

- Encourage viewers to reflect on how timing, holidays, or rituals have shaped their own experiences with loss.

Final Thought

Nora's Will shows how death can reopen old wounds while quietly offering the possibility of healing. Through ritual, obligation, and human connection, the film reminds us that, even in the most painful circumstances, care for the dead can become a profound act of care for the living.

The Six Wives of Henry Lefay *(2009, PG-13, 1 h 35 min)*

Starring: Tim Allen, Elisha Cuthbert, Andie MacDowell

Directed by: Howard Michael Gould

Film Description

When it appears that Henry Lefay died suddenly in Mexico, his adult daughter Barbara finds herself trying to arrange his funeral while navigating a small army of ex-wives, each convinced they know exactly what Henry would have wanted. As competing burial wishes, emotional baggage, and unresolved resentments collide, Barbara must make sense of her father's legacy with no clear plan to guide her. The result is a fast-moving comedy that uses chaos to underline a very real lesson about what happens when end-of-life plans are vague, outdated, or never shared.

Mortality Themes

- Funeral planning without clear instructions

- The consequences of not updating wishes after life changes

- Family conflict and blended-family dynamics after death

- Legacy, memory, and who gets to decide "what he wanted"

- The emotional burden placed on survivors

Discussion Prompts

1. How could Henry's situation have been avoided with clearer or updated planning?

2. Who should have authority over funeral decisions, and why?

3. How do unresolved relationships complicate both grief and logistics?

4. What responsibility do we have to survivors when making (or avoiding) end-of-life plans?

5. How does blended-family complexity change the emotional landscape of funeral planning and decision-making?

6. What conversations about death, remarriage, or changing relationships should be revisited over time rather than assumed to remain understood?

Movie Pairings and Activities

- Pair the movie with *Get Low* (2009) to compare proactive versus absent funeral planning.

- Or pair it with *Eulogy* (2004) for another look at family dysfunction erupting at funerals.

- Ask viewers to consider whether their own wishes are written down, updated, and shared with the right people.

Final Thought

The Six Wives of Henry Lefay plays funeral chaos for laughs, but the takeaway is serious: When plans are unclear, the living pay the price. The film is a reminder that thoughtful preparation is not about control after death. It's about sparing the people you love from confusion, conflict, and guesswork when they are already grieving.

Taking Chance *(2009, TV-PG, 1 h 17 min)*

Starring: Kevin Bacon

Directed by: Ross Katz

Film Description

Based on real-life events, *Taking Chance* follows Lieutenant Colonel Michael Strobl, a Marine officer, who volunteers to escort the body of nineteen-year-old Lance Corporal Chance Phelps from Dover Air Force Base to his hometown of Dubois, Wyoming. The film quietly traces the journey across the country, focusing on the rituals, logistics, and moments of human connection that arise along the way. With restraint and dignity, it shows how ordinary people participate, often wordlessly, in honoring a fallen service member.

Mortality Themes

- Military death rituals and honors
- The importance of witnessing death and remembrance
- Respect, dignity, and duty after death
- Collective mourning and national service
- Bearing witness as an act of meaning

Discussion Prompts

1. What does it mean to "bear witness" to death, and why does it matter?
2. How do military death rituals differ from civilian funerals, and what purpose do those differences serve?
3. What moments in the film show respect without words?
4. How does this journey affect the escort officer on a personal level?
5. How does public participation, even silent participation, contribute to collective mourning and national memory?
6. What responsibilities do institutions carry in ensuring dignity for the dead and support for the living?

Movie Pairings and Activities

- Pair the movie with *Last Flag Flying* (2017) to explore different military burial experiences.

- Or pair it with *Brian's Song* (1971) for another look at honor, loss, and public remembrance.

- Discuss the rituals of honor in different cultures or professions and how they help communities process loss.

Final Thought

Taking Chance is a quiet film, but its message resonates deeply: Death deserves to be seen, acknowledged, and honored. The line "Without a witness . . . it just disappears" captures the heart of the story. By showing us the care taken in this final journey, the film reminds us that remembrance is not passive. It is an act of presence, respect, and humanity.

This Is Where I Leave You *(2014, R, 1 h 43 min)*

Starring: Jason Bateman, Tina Fey, Jane Fonda, Adam Driver, Rose Byrne

Directed by: Shawn Levy

Film Description

After the death of their father, four adult siblings are compelled to return to their childhood home to sit shivah for seven days, as dictated by Jewish mourning tradition. Under the watchful eye of their candid, boundary-blurring mother, old resentments resurface, secrets spill out, and unresolved relationships collide. What begins as an obligation quickly becomes a pressure cooker of grief, humor, and reckoning.

Mortality Themes

- Ritualized mourning and sitting shivah

- Family dynamics during early grief

- Grief as a catalyst for growth and confrontation

- The tension between tradition and modern life

- How death forces stalled relationships into motion

Discussion Prompts

1. How does the structure of shivah shape the characters' grieving process?

2. In what ways does forced togetherness help or hinder healing?

3. How do humor and conflict coexist in this portrayal of grief?

4. What does the film suggest about the role of ritual after a death?

5. How does sitting shivah create both accountability and vulnerability among family members?

6. What unfinished conversations might be easier to begin during structured mourning time rather than months or years later?

Movie Pairings and Activities

*   Pair the movie with *My Mexican Shivah* (2007) for another culturally grounded look at mourning rituals.

*   Or pair it with *The Big Chill* (1983) to compare grief, reunion, and unresolved adulthood, in a secular shivah setting.

*   Discuss how different cultures create space for grief through ritual and time-bound mourning.

Final Thought

This Is Where I Leave You does not aim to teach the mechanics of Jewish mourning, but it excels at revealing the emotional truth beneath it. Grief is rarely tidy, families are rarely calm, and growth often happens amid discomfort. By trapping its characters together in mourning, the film reminds us that death does not just mark an ending; it stirs the living into change, whether they are ready or not.

Undertaking Betty *(2002, PG-13, 1 h 34 min)*

*(Originally released as **Plots with a View**)*

Starring: Brenda Blethyn, Alfred Molina, Christopher Walken

Directed by: Nick Hurran

Film Description

Set in a small Welsh village where tradition reigns supreme, *Undertaking Betty* centers on Betty, a long-suffering wife whose philandering husband has worn out her patience and everyone else's goodwill. Enter Frank Featherbed, a flamboyant forward-thinking funeral director from the United States who brings personalized funerals, theatrical flair, and unconventional ideas to a town accustomed to somber, cookie-cutter services. His arrival disrupts not only the local funeral industry but also Betty's life, especially as her quiet admirer, Boris Plots, the town's conservative undertaker, finally finds the courage to step out of the shadows.

Mortality Themes

- Traditional versus personalized funeral practices
- Funeral directors as agents of cultural change
- Celebration of life versus solemn ritual
- Community resistance to innovation around death
- Love, reinvention, and second chances

Discussion Prompts

1. Why do communities often resist changes in funeral traditions?
2. How does personalization in funerals help or challenge mourners?
3. What role do funeral directors play beyond logistics and ceremony?
4. How does humor make conversations about death more accessible?
5. How do economic pressures influence how funerals are designed and marketed?
6. What traditions feel essential to preserve, and which might benefit from thoughtful reinvention?

Movie Pairings and Activities

- Pair the movie with *Happy Funeral* (2008) for another cross-cultural look at reimagining funeral rituals.

- Or pair it with *The Loved One* (1965) to compare satire of the funeral industry across decades.

- Invite participants to design a "celebration of life" that reflects personality, values, or passions rather than tradition alone.

Final Thought

Undertaking Betty reminds us that funerals are not just about honoring the dead but about serving the living. By blending romance, farce, and mortuary mischief, the film gently argues that meaning matters more than rules and that a well-planned farewell can be heartfelt, healing, and, yes, even a little fun. As Frank Featherbed wisely notes, "Remember: The root word of 'funeral' is 'fun.'"

Waking Ned Devine *(1998, PG, 1 h 31 min)*

Starring: Ian Bannen, David Kelly, Fionnula Flanagan

Directed by: Kirk Jones

Film Description

In a tiny wind-swept Irish village where everyone knows everyone else's business, longtime friends Jackie and Michael discover that local bachelor Ned Devine has won the national lottery. Unfortunately, Ned dies from the shock of the news before he can claim the prize. Convinced that Ned would have wanted his neighbors to benefit from his good fortune, the townspeople hatch an audacious plan to convince lottery officials that Ned is still alive. What follows is a communal act of storytelling, solidarity, and quiet rebellion against rigid systems that fail to honor human connection.

Mortality Themes

- Community responsibility after death

- The meaning of legacy beyond money

- Being present and acknowledged while alive
- Funerals as spaces for truth-telling and reflection
- Collective grief transformed into collective care

Discussion Prompts

1. What does the film suggest about who truly "owns" a legacy after death?

2. How does community shape the way grief is expressed and shared?

3. Is the villagers' deception ethical or an act of moral justice?

4. What does the eulogy scene reveal about how we speak of the dead versus the living?

5. How does the village's collective decision blur the line between honoring a friend and serving their own interests?

6. What does the film suggest about expressing appreciation while someone is still alive rather than waiting for a funeral?

Movie Pairings and Activities

- Pair the movie with *Get Low* (2009) for another take on hearing one's own funeral while still alive.
- Or pair it with *Bernie* (2011) to explore community complicity and moral gray areas around death.
- Invite participants to write a short "living eulogy" for themselves or someone they admire, focusing on presence rather than praise.

Final Thought

Waking Ned Devine offers a gentle but powerful reminder that funerals are not just about endings but about witness. The film's most poignant insight comes in its reflection that "the words spoken at a funeral are too late for the man who has died." In celebrating Ned while bending the rules in his name, the villagers honor something deeper than money: belonging, remembrance, and the quiet hope that we might be truly seen before it's too late.

Funerals and Funeral Directors: Closing Thoughts

What these films ultimately show is that there is no single "right" way to hold a funeral, only honest ones. When rituals reflect the life that was lived, they can comfort, unite, and even transform the people left behind. When they do not, they often expose unresolved grief, family fractures, or the consequences of never having talked about death at all.

Funeral directors in these stories emerge not merely as service providers but as guides through unfamiliar terrain. At their best, they help families slow down, make informed choices, and find meaning amid chaos. At their worst, they reflect what happens when transparency and preparation are missing. Both versions are instructive.

If this chapter encourages readers to talk about funeral wishes, to learn their rights as consumers, or simply to view funerals with less fear and more curiosity, it has done its job. Planning for death does not diminish life. It clarifies it. And a well-considered goodbye can be one of the most generous gifts we leave behind.

MEDICAL TREATMENT AND END-OF-LIFE ISSUES

Introduction

Death may be universal, but the ways we approach the end of life, or avoid talking about it altogether, are as varied as the movies in this chapter. These films take us into hospital rooms, exam chairs, hospice suites, and the emotionally complex spaces where medicine, mortality, and humanity intersect. Some stories are quiet and intimate. Others are bold, unsettling, or darkly funny. A few use humor as a kind of anesthesia while delivering difficult truths.

What connects them is the opportunity they offer us as viewers. These films let us witness conversations many people are reluctant to have. They show what can go wrong when no one plans ahead and what can go surprisingly well when patients, families, and clinicians speak honestly and compassionately. Whether a character is grappling with a new diagnosis, seeking autonomy in how their life ends, or questioning the ethics of life-prolonging treatment, each story reminds us that end-of-life experiences are not just medical events; they are deeply human ones.

In recent years, conversations about medical aid in dying (MAID) have become more visible in both public discourse and popular culture. Some of the films in this chapter portray characters who consider or pursue this option. It is important to recognize that MAID is governed by specific laws that vary by jurisdiction, with strict eligibility requirements, procedural safeguards, and medical oversight where it is permitted.

Cinematic portrayals may simplify, dramatize, or alter those realities for storytelling purposes. Viewers are encouraged to approach these films as conversation starters rather than instructional guides. Consult current, reliable sources for up-to-date information about the law where you live. However one feels about it, medical aid in dying raises profound questions about autonomy, suffering, dignity, and how we define a "good death" in an era of advanced medical intervention.

Movies become a kind of rehearsal space. They allow us to explore emotions, values, and personal wishes from the safety of a couch, ideally with popcorn nearby. And if a film sparks an uncomfortable but necessary conversation afterward, that may be the most therapeutic outcome of all.

50/50 *(2010, R, 1 h 40 min)*

Starring: Joseph Gordon-Levitt, Seth Rogen, Anna Kendrick

Directed by: Jonathan Levine

Film Description

Inspired by a true story, *50/50* follows Adam Lerner, a twenty-seven-year-old radio producer, who is blindsided by a diagnosis of a rare form of cancer. Given a survival prognosis of "50/50," Adam must navigate chemotherapy, surgery, and the emotional whiplash that follows a life-altering medical conversation. The film balances humor and vulnerability as Adam contends with strained family dynamics, dating while ill, and well-meaning but often awkward support from friends. Seth Rogen plays Adam's best friend, whose attempts to help range from heartfelt to wildly inappropriate.

Mortality Themes

- The shock and dissociation that often follow a serious diagnosis
- Living with uncertain outcomes
- The emotional labor of illness placed on patients
- Friendship, caregiving, and mismatched support styles
- Youthful invincibility disrupted by mortality awareness
- Medical treatment as both lifesaving and dehumanizing

Discussion Prompts

1. How accurately does the film portray the moment of diagnosis and the emotional numbness that can follow?

2. In what ways do Adam's friends and family struggle to support him despite good intentions?

3. How does the film handle humor in the face of serious illness? When does it help, and when does it miss the mark?

4. What does *50/50* reveal about how society expects young people with cancer to behave or "stay positive"?

5. How does Adam's experience highlight gaps in emotional support within the medical system?

6. What does the film suggest about control, randomness, and acceptance when outcomes are uncertain?

Movie Pairings and Activities

- Pair the movie with *The Big Sick* (2017) for another humor-forward look at illness and intimacy.

- Or pair it with *Wit* (2001) for a starkly different, more clinical perspective on cancer treatment.

- Invite viewers to reflect on how they would want serious medical news delivered, including who should be present and what information matters the most in that moment.

Final Thought

50/50 succeeds because it does not turn cancer into a moral test or a sentimental journey. Instead, it shows illness as disruptive, unfair, and deeply human. By centering the emotional experience of a young patient rather than the drama of the disease itself, the film opens space for honest conversations about fear, friendship, and what it means to keep living when nothing feels guaranteed.

Blackbird *(2019, R, 1 h 37 min)*

Starring: Susan Sarandon, Sam Neill, Kate Winslet, Mia Wasikowska, Rainn Wilson

Directed by: Roger Michell

Film Description

In *Blackbird*, Lily, a woman living with a progressive neurodegenerative disease, gathers her family for one final weekend at their seaside home. With the support of her husband, she has decided to end her life through medical aid in dying before her illness fully robs her of autonomy and dignity. While Lily is clear and resolved in her decision, her family members are not, and long-standing tensions surface as each person grapples with grief, fear, love, and moral conflict.

Mortality Themes

- Medical aid in dying and patient autonomy
- Control, dignity, and timing at the end of life
- Anticipatory grief within families
- Conflicting values around choice, suffering, and responsibility
- The emotional impact of planned death versus sudden loss
- Communication, secrecy, and truth-telling at the end of life

Discussion Prompts

1. How does Lily define a "good death," and how does that differ from her family members' perspectives?

2. What emotions and fears drive the family's resistance to Lily's decision?

3. How does the film portray autonomy when it conflicts with the wishes of loved ones?

4. In what ways does planning the timing of death change the grieving process for those left behind?

5. How might this story have unfolded differently if Lily had not clearly communicated her wishes in advance?

6. Does the film challenge or reinforce your views on medical aid in dying?

Movie Pairings and Activities

- Pair the movie with *Still Alice* (2014) for a different exploration of cognitive decline and control.

- Or pair it with *Whose Life Is It Anyway?* (1981) for a courtroom-centered debate on autonomy and choice.

- Use the film as a springboard for discussing advance directives, values statements, or how families can talk about end-of-life wishes before a crisis occurs.

Final Thought

Blackbird does not argue for or against medical aid in dying. Instead, it places viewers inside the emotional reality of a family forced to confront love, fear, and loss on a fixed timeline. By focusing on relationships rather than ideology, the film reminds us that end-of-life decisions are never made in isolation and that autonomy, while deeply personal, is always felt collectively.

Brian's Song *(1971, G, TV movie, 1 h 13 min)*

Starring: James Caan, Billy Dee Williams, Jack Warden

Directed by: Buzz Kulik

Film Description

Based on a true story, *Brian's Song* chronicles the friendship between Chicago Bears teammates Brian Piccolo and Gale Sayers at a time when racial integration in professional football was still uncommon. Their bond deepens when Piccolo is diagnosed with an aggressive form of cancer. As his health declines, the film follows how both men, their families, and their team navigate illness, hope, and impending loss. Originally made for television, the film became a cultural touchstone for its honest portrayal of terminal illness and friendship.

Mortality Themes

- Terminal illness in young adulthood
- Friendship as a source of meaning and resilience
- Anticipatory grief and emotional vulnerability
- Masculinity and expressing fear, love, and sorrow
- The impact of death within teams and communities
- Legacy through relationships rather than achievements

Discussion Prompts

1. How does Brian Piccolo's illness change the way the characters relate to one another?

2. What makes this portrayal of male friendship feel emotionally powerful, especially for its time?

3. How does the film handle hope alongside realism about Piccolo's prognosis?

4. In what ways does Brian's youth intensify the emotional impact of his death?

5. How do Gale Sayers' experiences reflect the grief of those who survive a close friend?

6. What does the film suggest about how we remember people who die young?

Movie Pairings and Activities

- Pair the movie with *Love Story* (1970) for another early portrayal of terminal illness and young adulthood.

- Or pair it with *Terms of Endearment* (1983) to explore family dynamics alongside serious illness.

- Invite viewers to reflect on friendships that have shaped them and discuss how an illness or a loss can clarify what matters the most in relationships.

Final Thought

Brian's Song endures not because it avoids sentiment but because it earns it. By centering illness within a story of friendship, the film reminds us that death does not only take lives, it reshapes those who remain. Its lasting power lies in its simple truth: Love between people is often revealed most clearly when time is short.

Checking Out *(2005, PG-13, 1 h 34 min)*

Starring: Peter Falk, Laura San Giacomo, David Paymer

Directed by: Jeff Hare

Film Description

In this dark comedy, Peter Falk plays Morris Applebaum, an almost-ninety-year-old former stage actor, who believes he has lived long enough. As his family gathers to celebrate his milestone birthday, Morris reveals that he intends to end his life using a combination of alcohol and barbiturates. His announcement shocks his loved ones and sparks a range of reactions, from anger and denial to fear and compassion. The film uses humor to explore serious questions about aging, autonomy, and what it means to choose when life is "enough."

Mortality Themes

- Aging and perceived quality of life
- Suicide versus medical aid in dying
- Autonomy and control at the end of life
- Family conflict around end-of-life decisions
- Fear of decline and dependency
- Humor as a way to approach uncomfortable truths

Discussion Prompts

1. How does Morris define having lived "long enough," and how do others challenge that belief?

2.   What emotions drive the family's opposition to Morris' plan?

3.   How does the film distinguish, or blur, the line between suicide and end-of-life autonomy?

4.   In what ways does humor make these difficult conversations more accessible?

5.   How might this story differ if Morris were terminally ill rather than simply elderly?

6.   What responsibilities, if any, do families have when a loved one expresses a desire to die?

Movie Pairings and Activities

- Pair the movie with *Blackbird* (2019) for a more serious portrayal of medical aid in dying.

- Or pair it with *The Farewell* (2019) to contrast family-centered approaches to end-of-life truth-telling.

- Invite viewers to discuss what quality of life means to them personally and whether it can or should be defined in advance.

Final Thought

Checking Out walks a fine line between comedy and moral inquiry. While it does not offer easy answers, it succeeds in asking essential questions about aging, dignity, and who gets to decide when a life feels complete. Its greatest value lies in opening space for conversation, especially around choices many families hope they will never have to face.

Critical Care *(1997, R, 1 h 47 min)*

Starring: James Spader, Kyra Sedgwick, Helen Mirren, Albert Brooks

Directed by: Sidney Lumet

Film Description

This sharp-edged black comedy places James Spader in the role of Dr. Werner Ernst, a hospital resident, who suddenly finds himself caught between two half-sisters locked in a bitter dispute over their comatose father's care. One sister insists on keeping him alive at all costs, while the other is eager to end life support. As legal maneuvering, insurance pressures, and hospital politics swirl around the bedside, the patient himself becomes almost invisible. Directed by Sidney Lumet, the film satirizes modern medicine while exposing how financial incentives, ego, and family dysfunction can complicate life-and-death decisions in the ICU.

Mortality Themes

- Life support and end-of-life decision-making
- Family conflict and competing motivations
- Medical ethics versus financial incentives
- The dehumanization of patients in complex systems
- Power dynamics in hospital settings
- Moral distress among healthcare providers

Discussion Prompts

1. How do the sisters' motivations shape their positions on life support?
2. At what point does medical treatment become prolonging death rather than sustaining life?
3. How does the film portray the role of insurance and money in medical decision-making?
4. In what ways is the patient marginalized or objectified during the conflict?
5. How does humor function as both critique and discomfort in this film?
6. What responsibilities do physicians have when families are deeply divided?

Movie Pairings and Activities

- Pair the film with *Wit* (2001) for a patient-centered perspective on medical power.
- Or pair it with *Being Mortal* (Frontline) to ground the satire in real-world practice.

- Ask viewers to imagine themselves as the patient. What advance directives might prevent this kind of conflict?

Final Thought

Critical Care is intentionally unsettling. By exaggerating real tensions within the healthcare system, it forces viewers to confront uncomfortable truths about how decisions are made when patients can no longer speak for themselves. Its satire underscores a sobering message: Without clear communication and planning, end-of-life care can become more about control than compassion.

The Descendants *(2011, R, 1 h 55 min)*

Starring: George Clooney, Shailene Woodley, Amara Miller

Directed by: Alexander Payne

Film Description

George Clooney plays Matt King, a Honolulu attorney, whose life is abruptly upended when his wife Elizabeth is left in a coma after a boating accident. As she remains on life support with no chance of recovery, Matt must grapple with honoring her advance medical directives while simultaneously stepping into the unfamiliar role of primary caregiver to their two daughters. Complicating matters further, he learns of his wife's infidelity, forcing him to reconcile grief, anger, love, and loss all at once. Running parallel to the medical crisis is an estate dilemma involving a large tract of ancestral Hawaiian land, placing Matt at the intersection of personal loss, ethical responsibility, and cultural legacy.

Mortality Themes

- Life support and end-of-life decision-making
- Advance medical directives and honoring patient wishes
- Sudden illness and anticipatory grief
- Parenting through crisis and loss
- Complicated grief involving betrayal

- Inheritance, legacy, and stewardship of land
- Balancing family needs with cultural responsibility

Discussion Prompts

1. How does Elizabeth's advance directive guide the medical decisions in the film?

2. What emotional challenges arise when grief is complicated by anger or betrayal?

3. How does Matt's role as a father change in response to his wife's condition?

4. In what ways do clear medical conversations help or fail the family?

5. How do the estate issues mirror the themes of stewardship and responsibility at the end of life?

6. What support systems seem to help Matt cope, and where does he struggle alone?

Movie Pairings and Activities

- Pair the movie with *Wit* (2001) for another exploration of patient autonomy.
- Or pair it with *The Grand Budapest Hotel* (2014) to compare legacy and inheritance themes.
- Invite viewers to reflect on whether their own medical wishes are clearly documented and communicated.

Final Thought

The Descendants offers a layered portrait of end-of-life decision-making that extends beyond hospital walls. It reminds us that death often arrives tangled in unresolved relationships, unfinished conversations, and practical responsibilities. The film gently reinforces a crucial truth: Planning ahead does not remove pain, but it can offer clarity and compassion when families need it the most.

The Doctor *(1991, PG-13, 2 h 2 min)*

Starring: William Hurt, Christine Lahti

Directed by: Randa Haines

Film Description

William Hurt plays Dr. Jack McKee, a brilliant but emotionally detached cardiothoracic surgeon, whose life is upended when he is diagnosed with throat cancer. Accustomed to authority and control, Jack suddenly finds himself on the other side of the hospital gown, subjected to rushed appointments, dehumanizing procedures, and clinicians who treat his body but not his humanity. As he navigates surgery, radiation, and recovery, Jack's experience as a patient fundamentally reshapes how he understands suffering, vulnerability, and the ethical responsibilities of medical professionals.

Mortality Themes

- Illness as a catalyst for empathy and personal transformation
- The patient experience versus the clinician perspective
- Communication, dignity, and compassion in medical care
- Power dynamics within healthcare systems
- Identity disruption following a serious diagnosis
- Life reevaluation prompted by mortality awareness

Discussion Prompts

1. How does Jack's experience as a patient change the way he practices medicine?

2. What moments in the film best illustrate how patients can feel dehumanized in healthcare settings?

3. How does illness disrupt Jack's sense of identity and control?

4. What responsibilities do medical professionals have beyond clinical competence?

5. How might healthcare systems better balance efficiency with compassion?

6. In what ways does confronting mortality expand Jack's understanding of life beyond work?

Movie Pairings and Activities

- Pair the movie with *Wit* (2001) to compare clinician-patient power dynamics.

- Or pair it with *50/50* (2011) to explore illness from a younger patient's perspective.

- Invite participants to reflect on a healthcare encounter that made them feel either seen or invisible, and discuss what made the difference.

Final Thought

The Doctor remains a powerful reminder that medical expertise alone is not enough. By forcing its protagonist to confront illness from the patient's side, the film argues that empathy is not an optional add-on to care but an essential part of healing. Mortality, it suggests, is often the teacher that medicine itself forgets to be.

The End *(1978, R, 1 h 40 min)*

Starring: Burt Reynolds, Dom DeLuise, Sally Field

Directed by: Burt Reynolds

Film Description

This dark slapstick comedy follows Sonny Lawson (Burt Reynolds), a successful businessman, who is told by his doctor that he has a terminal illness and little time left to live. Overwhelmed by fear, anger, and self-pity, Sonny embarks on a series of increasingly chaotic and unsuccessful suicide attempts. After landing in a psychiatric facility, he befriends Marlon (Dom DeLuise), an enthusiastic but deeply unqualified would-be assistant, who tries to help Sonny "get it right." While played for broad laughs, the film traces Sonny's emotional volatility as he cycles through denial, rage, bargaining, and despair, without ever fully arriving at acceptance.

Mortality Themes

- Fear-based responses to terminal diagnosis
- Suicide ideation framed through dark comedy
- Psychological distress following medical news
- The inadequacy of impulsive decision-making at the end of life
- Mental health, institutionalization, and social discomfort with death
- The difference between wanting death and wanting relief from fear

Discussion Prompts

1. How does humor function in this film when addressing suicide and terminal illness?
2. What emotional stages does Sonny cycle through after his diagnosis?
3. How does the film portray medical communication and its impact on patients?
4. In what ways does Sonny confuse fear of dying with a desire to die?
5. Does the comedy help or hinder meaningful engagement with end-of-life issues?
6. How might this story differ if Sonny had access to hospice care or supportive counseling?

Movie Pairings and Activities

- Pair the movie with *50/50* (2010) to contrast fear-driven reactions with resilience.
- Or pair it with *Checking Out* (2005) to explore autonomy versus impulsivity at end of life.
- Invite discussion about how humor is used personally to cope with fear and where humor crosses into avoidance.

Final Thought

The End uses exaggerated comedy to expose a very real truth: Receiving a serious diagnosis can unravel a person emotionally long before death itself arrives. While Sonny never reaches acceptance, the film illustrates how fear, misinformation, and isolation can drive people toward desperate conclusions. Beneath the slapstick lies a cautionary tale about the importance of support, honest conversation, and addressing the emotional dimensions of mortality, not just the medical ones.

The Fault in Our Stars *(2014, PG-13, 2 h 6 min)*

Starring: Shailene Woodley, Ansel Elgort, Laura Dern, Willem Dafoe

Directed by: Josh Boone

Film Description

Based on the best-selling novel by John Green, this romantic drama centers on Hazel Grace Lancaster and Augustus Waters, two teenagers living with cancer, who meet in a support group and form a deep, witty, and emotionally honest connection. Aware that their lives may be short, they resist being defined solely by illness and instead pursue love, meaning, humor, and agency. One of the film's most memorable moments occurs when Augustus stages a "pre-funeral," asking Hazel and a close friend to speak about him while he is still alive, allowing him to witness his own legacy.

Mortality Themes

- Adolescent and young adult mortality
- Living fully while facing life-limiting illness
- Love and intimacy shaped by an awareness of death
- Legacy, remembrance, and the desire to be known
- Anticipatory grief for patients and caregivers
- Identity beyond diagnosis

Discussion Prompts

1. How does the film portray the tension between hope and realism for young people with a serious illness?

2. What does Augustus' living funeral reveal about the human desire for meaning and acknowledgment?

3. How do Hazel and Augustus negotiate love while knowing their time together may be limited?

4. In what ways does the film challenge cultural discomfort with talking openly about death?

5. How does illness affect independence, relationships, and self-image for young patients?

6. What lessons does the film offer about legacy that are not dependent on longevity?

Movie Pairings and Activities

- Pair the movie with *50/50* (2011) for a comparison of humor and youth in serious illness.

- Or pair it with *Love Story* (1970) to explore romantic love in the face of terminal diagnosis.

- Invite participants to write or discuss what they would want said at their own funeral and whether hearing it while alive would change how they live now.

Final Thought

The Fault in Our Stars reminds us that mortality does not diminish love; it intensifies it. By centering young voices and refusing sentimentality, the film invites honest conversations about death without stripping life of joy. It suggests that legacy is not measured in the years lived but in the depth of connection and the courage to love fully, even when time is uncertain.

Me and Earl and the Dying Girl *(2015, PG-13, 1 h 45 min)*

Starring: Thomas Mann, RJ Cyler, Olivia Cooke, Nick Offerman, Connie Britton

Directed by: Alfonso Gomez-Rejon

Film Description

This offbeat coming-of-age dark comedy follows Greg Gaines, a self-protective high school senior, who prides himself on being invisible. Along with his friend Earl, he spends his free time making irreverent parodies of classic films. When Greg's mother insists he befriend Rachel, a classmate diagnosed with leukemia, he reluctantly enters a relationship that challenges his emotional detachment. Rather than following familiar cancer-movie tropes, the film uses humor, storytelling, and subversion to explore how young people grapple with illness, mortality, and the fear of genuine connection.

Mortality Themes

- Serious illness during adolescence
- Emotional avoidance and anticipatory grief
- Storytelling as a coping mechanism
- Friendship and connection in the face of loss
- The limits of humor when confronting death
- Letting go of control and expectations

Discussion Prompts

1. How does the film deliberately resist traditional "inspirational" illness narratives?

2. In what ways does Greg use humor and filmmaking to distance himself from grief?

3. How does the movie portray the discomfort many people feel around someone who is dying?

4. What role does storytelling play in helping characters process fear and loss?

5. How does Rachel assert agency in how she wants to be seen and remembered?

6. What does the film suggest about the importance of showing up even when we feel inadequate?

Movie Pairings and Activities

- Pair the film with *The Fault in Our Stars* (2014) to contrast emotional tone and narrative expectations.

- Or pair it with *50/50* (2011) for another humor-inflected look at serious illness.

- Invite participants to reflect on how they personally use humor, art, or storytelling to cope with uncomfortable emotions, especially around illness or death.

Final Thought

Me and Earl and the Dying Girl refuses easy catharsis. Instead, it offers a more honest portrait of how awkward, imperfect, and unresolved our encounters with death often are. By letting the story remain messy and unresolved, the film reminds us that there is no "right" way to face mortality, only the choice to connect, even when it hurts.

The Room Next Door *(2024, PG-13, 1 h 47 min)*

Starring: Julianne Moore, Tilda Swinton

Directed by: Pedro Almodóvar

Film Description

In this intimate drama, two longtime friends, Ingrid and Martha, reunite under difficult circumstances. One is dying of cancer and has decided to pursue medical aid in dying. The other, while deeply devoted, is profoundly uncomfortable with death and uncertain how to accompany her friend through this choice. Much of the film unfolds in quiet conversations, shared spaces, and moments of emotional restraint, emphasizing the psychological and relational dimensions of end-of-life decision-making.

Rather than focusing on medical procedures, the film centers on the emotional labor of witnessing another person's death, particularly when beliefs about autonomy, fear, and mortality do not align. The tension between acceptance and resistance becomes the emotional core of the story.

The film's portrayal of medical aid in dying does not accurately reflect how the process functions in jurisdictions where it is legal. The method depicted in the story differs from current U.S. medical protocols, which involve strict eligibility criteria, physician oversight, and carefully regulated prescribing procedures. As with many films, dramatic storytelling takes precedence over legal and medical precision.

At the time of publication, medical aid in dying laws vary by state. In New York, where the story is set, legislation was approved in 2025 and is scheduled to take effect in August 2026. Readers are encouraged to consult up-to-date, reliable sources for current laws and requirements in their own state.

Mortality Themes

- Medical aid in dying
- Fear of death versus acceptance
- Friendship at the end of life
- Autonomy and consent
- Bearing witness to another's dying
- Emotional boundaries and moral discomfort

Discussion Prompts

1. How does the film portray differing responses to death between the two friends?
2. What responsibilities do loved ones have when they disagree with an end-of-life choice?
3. How does fear of death shape behavior, even in compassionate relationships?
4. What does the film suggest about accompaniment versus agreement?
5. How do silence and restraint function as emotional language in the story?
6. In what ways does the setting amplify the intimacy of the situation?

Movie Pairings and Activities

- Pair the movie with *Blackbird* (2019) or *Still Alice* (2014) to compare portrayals of autonomy and anticipatory grief.
- Invite viewers to reflect on how they would want a loved one to show up for them at the end of life even if values differ.

Final Thought

The Room Next Door is a quiet but piercing meditation on what it means to love someone who is dying when you are not ready to face death yourself. It reminds us that end-of-life care is not only about choices made by the dying but about the courage required of those who stay close even when fear is present.

The Savages *(2007, R, 1 h 53 min)*

Starring: Laura Linney, Philip Seymour Hoffman

Directed by: Tamara Jenkins

Film Description

This understated comedy-drama follows estranged siblings Wendy and Jon Savage who are forced back into each other's lives when their father develops dementia and can no longer live independently. After the death of his longtime partner, they bring him from Arizona to New York and confront the unfamiliar terrain of nursing homes, declining cognition, medical decision-making, and unresolved family history. The film resists sentimentality, instead offering a realistic portrait of adult children navigating caregiving, guilt, resentment, and responsibility.

Mortality Themes

- Dementia and cognitive decline
- Role reversal between parents and adult children
- Advance healthcare directives and decision-making
- Institutional care and quality of life
- Complicated family dynamics and unresolved grief
- Emotional distance as a coping mechanism

Discussion Prompts

1. How does the film portray the emotional burden of caring for an aging parent with dementia?

2. In what ways do Wendy and Jon avoid difficult conversations, and what are the consequences?

3. How does the lack of advance planning shape the siblings' experience?

4. What does the film suggest about responsibility versus obligation in family caregiving?

5. How do humor and detachment function as survival tools in this story?

6. What moments reveal compassion emerging despite long-standing estrangement?

Movie Pairings and Activities

- Pair the film with *Still Alice* (2014) for a patient-centered look at dementia.

- Or pair it with *Away from Her* (2006) for a spousal perspective on cognitive decline.

- Encourage viewers to reflect on what conversations they would want to have before a health crisis arises. This can include advance directives, care preferences, or values around quality of life.

Final Thought

The Savages captures a truth many families recognize: End-of-life care is rarely graceful, emotionally tidy, or redemptive. Yet within the awkward silences and imperfect decisions, the film finds something quietly human. Even fractured families can show up, imperfectly, when mortality makes avoidance impossible.

The Shootist *(1976, PG, 1 h 40 min)*

Starring: John Wayne, Jimmy Stewart, Lauren Bacall, John Carradine

Directed by: Don Siegel

Film Description

Set in 1901, this unusual Western follows aging gunfighter John Bernard Books who rides into Carson City seeking confirmation of a prostate cancer diagnosis. A man who has lived by violence, Books now faces death with clear-eyed pragmatism. With limited medical options available, he focuses on managing pain, preserving dignity, and controlling how his life will end. Along the way, he forms a bond with a widow and her son, confronts his violent legacy, and makes advance arrangements with the local undertaker.

This was John Wayne's final film before he died of lung cancer. The parallels between the actor and this character add an additional layer of resonance.

Mortality Themes

- Terminal illness and acceptance of death
- Pain management and quality of life
- Dignity at the end of life
- Advance funeral planning
- Limited medical interventions in historical context
- Legacy, reputation, and reconciliation

Discussion Prompts

1. How does John Books define dignity at the end of life?
2. What does the film suggest about control and autonomy when medicine offers few options?
3. How do Books' advance funeral arrangements reflect his values?
4. In what ways does the historical setting clarify or complicate end-of-life decisions?
5. How does the knowledge of John Wayne's real-life illness shape your viewing of the film?
6. What role does reconciliation, or lack of it, play in Books' final days?

Movie Pairings and Activities

- Pair the movie with *Ikiru* (1952) for another story of a man confronting mortality with intention.
- Or pair it with *Gran Torino* (2008) for a modern Western-inflected reflection on legacy and death.

- Invite viewers to consider what "dying with dignity" means to them. What elements would matter the most: pain control, location, relationships, or how one is remembered?

Final Thought

The Shootist strips the Western hero of myth and bravado, leaving behind a man confronting the most universal reckoning. In doing so, it reminds us that courage at the end of life is not found in how loudly we fight death but in how thoughtfully we prepare for it.

Still Alice *(2014, PG-13, 1 h 41 min)*

Starring: Julianne Moore, Alec Baldwin, Kristen Stewart, Kate Bosworth

Directed by: Richard Glatzer and Wash Westmoreland

Film Description

Alice Howland is a renowned linguistics professor whose life is upended when she is diagnosed with early-onset Alzheimer's disease. As her cognitive abilities gradually decline, Alice confronts the loss of identity that precedes physical death. She attempts to remain engaged with her work, her marriage, and her children even as the disease steadily erodes her independence.

One of the film's most striking moments occurs when Alice records instructions for herself on how to end her life before the disease progresses too far. This scene, quiet and deeply unsettling, opens space for conversations about autonomy, fear of dependency, and the ethical complexity surrounding end-of-life decisions.

Mortality Themes

- Loss of identity before physical death
- Anticipatory grief
- Cognitive decline and dignity
- End-of-life planning and autonomy
- Caregiver burden and family strain
- The emotional impact of terminal neurological illness

Discussion Prompts

1. How does Alice define herself, and how does the disease challenge that identity?

2. What emotions are evoked by Alice's recorded plan for ending her life?

3. How does the film portray anticipatory grief for both the patient and her family?

4. In what ways do Alice's family members cope differently with her diagnosis?

5. How does the film complicate the idea of autonomy when cognition is declining?

6. What conversations does this film invite families to have earlier rather than later?

Movie Pairings and Activities

- Pair the film with *Away From Her* (2006) or *The Savages* (2007) to compare portrayals of dementia and family caregiving.

- Invite viewers to reflect on what aspects of selfhood matter the most to them. How might those values influence advance directives or care preferences?

Final Thought

Still Alice confronts a form of dying that unfolds in slow motion where the self slips away long before the body does. It asks us to consider not only how long we live but how we define living and who we want beside us as memory, language, and certainty begin to fade.

Terms of Endearment *(1983, PG, 2 h 12 min)*

Starring: Shirley MacLaine, Debra Winger, Jack Nicholson, Danny DeVito

Directed by: James L. Brooks

Film Description

This comedy drama traces decades in the emotionally charged relationship between Aurora Greenway and her daughter Emma Horton. What begins as a story about love, marriage, and generational tension takes a profound turn when Emma is diagnosed with terminal cancer. The final act of the film unfolds largely in hospital settings, where issues of pain management, communication with medical professionals, and family dynamics under extreme stress take center stage.

The film is particularly remembered for its unflinching portrayal of a mother advocating fiercely for her dying child, capturing both the desperation and the courage that often surface in medical crises. While moments of humor persist, the story does not soften the realities of suffering, anticipatory grief, and the limits of medicine.

Mortality Themes

- Serious illness and terminal diagnosis
- Pain management and patient advocacy
- Anticipatory grief
- Parent-child bonds under stress
- Emotional labor of caregiving
- Death within the family system

Discussion Prompts

1. How does the mother-daughter relationship evolve as Emma's illness progresses?

2. What does the film suggest about advocacy in medical settings?

3. How are humor and anger used as coping mechanisms in the face of impending loss?

4. In what ways do the hospital scenes reflect real-world challenges families face during end-of-life care?

5. How does the film portray the tension between hope and acceptance?

6. What moments feel the most authentic in depicting grief before death occurs?

Movie Pairings and Activities

- Pair the film with *Steel Magnolias* (1989) or *Beaches* (1988) for additional explorations of female relationships and terminal illness.

- Discuss how families can prepare for medical advocacy roles. What questions should be asked, and who should speak when a loved one cannot?

Final Thought

Terms of Endearment endures because it refuses to sentimentalize illness or grief. It captures the raw, imperfect ways families love each other through suffering, reminding us that end-of-life care is not only about medicine but about voice, presence, and fiercely holding on to connection until the very end.

Two Weeks *(2006, R, 1 h 42 min)*

Starring: Sally Field, Ben Chaplin, Julianne Nicholson, Glenn Howerton

Directed by: Steve Stockman

Film Description

In this family-centered comedy drama, four adult siblings gather at their childhood home in North Carolina as their mother enters the final stage of her life on hospice care. Each arrives carrying old resentments, unresolved roles, and very different coping styles. Over the course of two weeks, caregiving duties, emotional reckonings, and practical end-of-life decisions collide in often awkward, sometimes tender ways.

The film offers a realistic depiction of home hospice, including the exhaustion of caregiving, the difficulty of clear communication, and the emotional whiplash families experience when death is imminent but unpredictable. A subplot involving the scattering of ashes underscores how even well-intentioned plans can go sideways when grief, logistics, and family dynamics intersect.

Mortality Themes

- Home hospice care
- Family caregiving stress
- Anticipatory grief
- Sibling dynamics during end-of-life care
- Practical end-of-life planning
- Memorialization and ash scattering mishaps

Discussion Prompts

1. How does each sibling cope differently with their mother's dying?
2. What does the film reveal about the emotional toll of family caregiving?
3. How realistically is hospice care portrayed in a home setting?
4. Where do unspoken family roles resurface under stress?
5. What can go wrong when end-of-life wishes are not clearly discussed?
6. How does humor function as both relief and avoidance in the film?

Movie Pairings and Activities

- Pair the movie with *The Savages* (2007) or *Terms of Endearment* (1983) for contrasting family caregiving experiences.
- Invite viewers to discuss who would realistically take on caregiving roles in their own families and what support they might need.

Final Thought

Two Weeks captures the messy middle ground of dying at home where love, fatigue, irritation, and devotion coexist. It reminds us that hospice care is as much about tending to family relationships as it is about caring for the person who is dying.

Whose Life Is It Anyway? *(1981, R, 1 h 59 min)*

Starring: Richard Dreyfuss, John Cassavetes, Christine Lahti

Directed by: John Badham

Film Description

Richard Dreyfuss stars as Ken Harrison, a successful sculptor, whose life changes irrevocably after a car accident leaves him paralyzed from the neck down. Though physically dependent on machines and caregivers, Ken remains mentally sharp, articulate, and fully aware of his condition. Concluding that his quality of life is unacceptable to him, he asks to be allowed to die.

When the hospital refuses his request, Ken's case becomes a legal and ethical battle that moves into the courtroom. Doctors, administrators, lawyers, and judges debate whether competence grants a person the right to refuse life-sustaining treatment, or whether the medical system has an obligation to preserve life at all costs. The film places patient autonomy, bodily integrity, and medical paternalism under a bright and uncomfortable spotlight.

Mortality Themes

- Quality of life versus quantity of life
- Patient autonomy and informed consent
- Disability and assumptions about worth
- Medical ethics and life-sustaining treatment
- Legal authority versus personal choice
- Control, dignity, and identity after catastrophic injury

Discussion Prompts

1. How does the film define "quality of life," and who gets to decide?
2. In what ways do the medical staff project their own fears or values onto Ken?
3. How does the courtroom setting change the discussion about dying?
4. What role does mental competence play in end-of-life decision-making?

5. Does the film challenge or reinforce assumptions about disability?

6. What emotions arise when autonomy conflicts with professional duty?

Movie Pairings and Activities

- Pair the film with *Million Dollar Baby* (2004) or *Still Alice* (2014) for additional perspectives on autonomy and identity.

- Invite participants to reflect on where they draw personal lines around independence, dignity, and acceptable quality of life.

Final Thought

Whose Life Is It Anyway? refuses to offer easy answers. Instead, it insists that the most uncomfortable questions about dying deserve to be asked directly and that listening to the person whose life is at stake is not just compassionate but essential.

Wit *(2001, PG-13, 1 h 39 min)*

Starring: Emma Thompson, Christopher Lloyd, Audra McDonald

Directed by: Mike Nichols

Based on: The Pulitzer Prize–winning play by Margaret Edson

Film Description

Emma Thompson delivers an extraordinary performance as Dr. Vivian Bearing, a renowned professor of English literature, who is diagnosed with stage IV ovarian cancer. Confident in intellect but emotionally guarded, Vivian consents to an aggressive experimental treatment regimen at a teaching hospital, believing she can endure it through sheer will and wit.

As the film unfolds, Vivian becomes less a person and more a subject of study. She experiences repeated indignities at the hands of a medical system focused on data, outcomes, and professional advancement rather than comfort or compassion. Breaking the fourth wall, Vivian addresses the audience directly, offering sharp observations, dark humor, and growing vulnerability as her illness progresses.

Through poetry, memory, and human connection, *Wit* examines what matters the most at the end of life. It becomes a powerful meditation on dignity, kindness, and the difference between treating disease and caring for a person.

Mortality Themes

- Loss of dignity within medical systems
- Experimental treatment and informed consent
- Patient vulnerability and power imbalance
- Compassion versus clinical detachment
- End-of-life wishes and comfort-focused care
- Identity beyond intellect and achievement

Discussion Prompts

1. How does Vivian's role shift from respected professor to medical subject?
2. What moments illustrate the difference between curing and caring?
3. How does a teaching hospital environment affect patient experience?
4. Why is the presence of kindness so transformative near the end of life?
5. What does the film suggest about how we measure a life well lived?
6. How might advance care planning have changed Vivian's experience?

Movie Pairings and Activities

- Pair the movie with *The Doctor* (1991) or *Still Alice* (2014) for additional perspectives on patient experience and dignity.
- Invite participants to reflect on what forms of care they would prioritize if cure were no longer possible.

Final Thought

Wit is both devastating and humane. It reminds us that brilliance offers little protection at the end of life but kindness offers everything. In stripping away pretense and power, the film asks us to consider how we want to be treated when all that remains is our humanity.

Medical Treatment and End-of-Life Issues: Closing Thoughts

If this chapter has shown us anything, it is that dying, much like living, is rarely tidy. People do not always agree. Medicine cannot always fix what is broken. Emotions do not follow a neat treatment plan. Yet within these stories lie blueprints for courage: the courage to talk openly about our wishes, to advocate for compassionate care, to let humor lighten even the heaviest moments, and to recognize when quality of life matters more than quantity.

These films invite us to see the end of life not as a medical failure but as a natural phase deserving clarity, honesty, and love. They remind us that advance directives are acts of kindness, that difficult conversations can spare families from heartbreaking guesswork, and that saying goodbye can be as meaningful as any other milestone in a life well lived.

If you finish this chapter feeling a tug to put your own wishes in writing, or to talk with someone you care about, consider that a cinematic prescription well filled. After all, the final chapter of our lives belongs to us, and the sooner we shape it, the better the story becomes.

DEATH FANTASY AND AFTERLIFE VISIONS

Introduction

Cinema has always been fascinated with the question none of us can avoid: *What happens next?*

This chapter explores the imaginative worlds that bloom where certainty ends. Here, filmmakers lean into the mystical, whimsical, eerie, or existential possibilities of what might happen when our story on Earth concludes. The afterlife becomes a playground for big questions: What happens next? Whom do we meet? What do we regret? What unfinished business follows us?

Whether death appears as a bureaucrat, a seductress, a best friend, a chess opponent, or a confused traveler between worlds, these films engage our curiosity about consciousness, continuity, justice, love, and legacy. They're creative invitations to consider that death may not be an ending but a transformation.

All That Jazz *(1979, R, 2 h 3 min)*

Starring: Roy Scheider, Jessica Lange, Ann Reinking, Leland Palmer

Directed by: Bob Fosse

Film Description

Loosely based on the life of legendary director and choreographer Bob Fosse, *All That Jazz* follows Joe Gideon, a brilliant self-destructive Broadway choreographer, who lives at full throttle. Joe juggles rehearsals, editing rooms, pills, cigarettes, women, and ego while ignoring the mounting warnings from his own body. Throughout the film, he engages in seductive, darkly playful conversations with Angelique, a glamorous figure, who represents death itself. As Joe's health collapses, reality and fantasy blur, culminating in a dazzling final musical number that reframes dying as the ultimate curtain call. The famous refrain "It's showtime!" becomes both bravado and denial in the face of mortality.

Mortality Themes

- Death as a constant companion rather than a distant event
- Denial, avoidance, and bargaining in the face of declining health
- Workaholism and identity fused with productivity
- The seduction of self-destruction and the cost of unchecked ambition
- Performance, legacy, and fantasies of a "good death"

Discussion Prompts

1. Joe Gideon is fully aware that his lifestyle is killing him. Why does awareness alone fail to change his behavior?

2. How does the character of Angelique shape our understanding of death? Is she comforting, dangerous, honest, or all three?

3. In what ways does Joe treat work as a way to avoid deeper emotional reckoning?

4. The final musical number turns death into a spectacle. Is this empowering, evasive, or both?

5. How does the film challenge the idea that dying should be solemn, quiet, or private?

6. What does *All That Jazz* suggest about the stories we tell ourselves to make dying feel acceptable or meaningful?

Movie Pairings and Activities

- Pair the film with *The Seventh Seal* (1958) for contrasting portrayals of death as a character.
- Or pair it with *Birdman* (2014) for another meditation on ego, legacy, and performance.

- Invite viewers to write their own "final number" in metaphor only, not what they would want to perform but how they would want their life to be remembered. Then discuss how close (or far) current choices feel from that vision.

Final Thought

All That Jazz refuses to moralize Joe Gideon's choices. Instead, it holds up a mirror to the ways brilliance, charisma, and productivity can distract us from listening to our bodies and our limits. The film asks an uncomfortable question: If death is always waiting in the wings, how much of our lives do we spend rehearsing instead of truly living? Joe's answer is a spectacle. The audience is left to decide whether that's enough.

Always *(1989, PG, 2 h 2 min)*

Starring: Richard Dreyfuss, Holly Hunter, John Goodman

Directed by: Steven Spielberg

Film Description

A remake of the 1943 fantasy *A Guy Named Joe*, *Always* tells the story of Pete Sandich, a daring aerial firefighter, whose life ends suddenly in the line of duty. Pete doesn't quite move on. Instead, he returns as a disembodied spirit assigned to mentor a talented but reckless young pilot. While guiding his successor, Pete must also watch Dorinda, the woman he loved, grieve his death and slowly fall in love again. With gentle humor and romantic longing, the film explores what it means to let go when love continues after death. The afterlife here is not grand or judgmental but quiet, purposeful, and rooted in unfinished emotional business.

Mortality Themes

- Sudden and accidental death
- Lingering spirits and unfinished business
- Love that continues beyond death
- Jealousy, attachment, and the challenge of letting go

- Legacy through mentorship rather than possession
- Rebirth and renewal following grief

Discussion Prompts

1. Pete struggles to accept that Dorinda will love again. Why is this such a common fear among the bereaved and the dying?

2. How does the film portray the afterlife as a place of responsibility rather than reward or punishment?

3. What does mentoring the younger pilot allow Pete to accomplish that he could not do in life?

4. Is Pete's lingering presence helpful or obstructive to Dorinda's healing?

5. How does *Always* distinguish between love and ownership?

6. What does the film suggest about holding on becoming an act of love and letting go becoming one?

Movie Pairings and Activities

- Pair the film with *Ghost* (1990) for another take on love and unfinished business after death.

- Or pair it with *Truly, Madly, Deeply* (1990) for a more emotionally complicated ghost story.

- Ask viewers to reflect on what kind of legacy they would want to leave if their role shifted from participant to mentor. Whom might they guide, and how?

Final Thought

Always presents death not as an ending but as a transition from center stage to supporting role. Pete's journey reminds us that love does not require proximity and devotion does not mean preventing others from moving forward. Sometimes the most meaningful goodbye is the one that clears space for life to continue.

Beetlejuice *(1988, PG, 1 h 32 min)*

Starring: Michael Keaton, Geena Davis, Alec Baldwin, Winona Ryder, Catherine O'Hara

Directed by: Tim Burton

Film Description

Tim Burton's gleefully macabre comedy begins with the sudden deaths of Adam and Barbara Maitland, a gentle newlywed couple, who die in a car accident and find themselves stuck haunting the beloved home they renovated. Armed with a *Handbook for the Recently Deceased* and very little confidence, they struggle to navigate their new afterlife status. When the aggressively living Deetz family moves in, the Maitlands attempt to scare them away, fail miserably, and summon the wildly untrustworthy bio-exorcist Beetlejuice. What follows is a riotous exploration of death as bureaucracy, grief as confusion, and the living and dead awkwardly negotiating space, control, and meaning.

Mortality Themes

- Sudden and accidental death
- Disorientation and identity after death
- Afterlife as bureaucracy and learning curve
- Attachment to home, possessions, and unfinished business
- Adolescent grief and death curiosity (Lydia)
- Control, consent, and vulnerability after death

Discussion Prompts

1. Adam and Barbara barely process their deaths before being thrust into "afterlife logistics." How does this mirror early grief experiences?

2. The afterlife in *Beetlejuice* is confusing, rule bound, and inefficient. What real-world systems does this parody?

3. Why are the Maitlands so attached to their house even after death? What might this say about legacy and fear of being erased?

4. Lydia feels more comfortable with the dead than the living. How does the film use her character to explore loneliness and adolescent grief?

5. Beetlejuice promises help but repeatedly violates boundaries. What does the film suggest about desperation and bad decision-making during vulnerable times?

6. How does humor make this film approachable even though its core subject is death?

Movie Pairings and Activities

- Pair the movie with *Death Becomes Her* (1992) for another darkly comic look at immortality.

- Or pair it with *Defending Your Life* (1991) for a more orderly after-life vision.

- Invite viewers to design their own "Handbook for the Recently Deceased" or "Recently Bereaved." What chapters would be most helpful in the first week after death?

Final Thought

Beetlejuice dresses mortality in stripes, slime, and slapstick, but beneath the chaos is a surprisingly thoughtful meditation on how disorienting death can be for everyone involved. It reminds us that death does not magically grant wisdom or closure and that navigating what comes next often requires patience, humility, and a firm refusal to summon anyone named Beetlejuice.

Bruce Almighty *(2003, PG-13, 1 h 41 min)*

Starring: Jim Carrey, Jennifer Aniston, Morgan Freeman

Directed by: Tom Shadyac

Film Description

Bruce Nolan is a talented but chronically dissatisfied television reporter who believes life has dealt him a raw deal. When he angrily blames God for all that's wrong in his life, God shows up in human form and hands Bruce divine powers, inviting him to see if he can do the job any better. What begins as a wish-fulfillment comedy quickly turns into a parable about responsibility, humility, and the unintended consequences of unchecked control. Beneath the laughs, the film nudges viewers to consider fate, free will, and what it means to live a meaningful life in a finite world.

Mortality Themes

- Human frustration with suffering and injustice
- Free will versus divine or cosmic order
- The limits of control and power
- Responsibility for others' well-being
- Making sense of ordinary life
- Humility in the face of forces larger than ourselves

Discussion Prompts

1. Bruce believes happiness will come once he has power and control. How does the film challenge that assumption?

2. What does *Bruce Almighty* suggest about free will? Is God portrayed as someone controlling outcomes or offering choices?

3. Bruce initially uses his powers for personal gain. How does this reflect common reactions to fear, insecurity, or dissatisfaction with life?

4. How does the film portray suffering? Is it something to be eliminated, avoided, or understood?

5. Morgan Freeman's god emphasizes small acts of kindness and presence. How does this contrast with more dramatic ideas of divine intervention?

6. How might this film open conversations about acceptance, gratitude, and living well within life's limits?

Movie Pairings and Activities

- Pair the movie with *Oh, God!* (1977) for a gentler conversational take on divinity.

- Or pair it with *Defending Your Life* (1991) for questions about moral accountability after death.

- Invite viewers to write a short list titled "If I Had God's Power for One Day…." Then reflect on what those wishes reveal about values, fears, and priorities.

Final Thought

Bruce Almighty wraps big spiritual questions in broad comedy, but its lasting message is quietly profound: Meaning is not found in omnipotence but in compassion, responsibility, and choosing to show up for one another. It reminds us that, even without divine powers, the way we live still matters.

Chances Are *(1989, PG, 1 h 48 min)*

Starring: Robert Downey Jr., Cybill Shepherd, Mary Stuart Masterson, Ryan O'Neal

Directed by: Emile Ardolino

Film Description

This romantic comedy with a supernatural twist opens with the sudden death of Louie Jeffries, a devoted husband, who is whisked through Heaven and reincarnated decades later as Alex Finch. As an adult, Alex begins to recover fragments of his former life, including a deep emotional pull toward Corinne, his wife from that earlier incarnation. Complications arise when he also forms a romantic connection with Miranda, Corinne's daughter from that first marriage, leading to some famously uncomfortable moments. Beneath the rom-com gloss, the film explores grief, memory, and the challenge of letting the past remain in the past.

Mortality Themes

- Reincarnation as an afterlife possibility

- Love that transcends a single lifetime

- Memory and identity after death

- Grief that lingers long after loss

- The necessity of letting go and moving forward

- The tension between second chances and unfinished business

Discussion Prompts

1. How does the film's portrayal of reincarnation compare with other cinematic visions of the afterlife?

2. Corinne mourns Louie for decades. How does the film depict long-term grief and its transformation over time?

3. What role does memory play in shaping identity in this story? Would remembering a past life be a gift or a burden?

4. The film uses humor to address an ethically complicated territory. Does comedy make these themes easier to engage with, or does it distract from them?

5. What does *Chances Are* suggest about the difference between honoring the past and trying to reclaim it?

6. How does the ending reinforce the idea that love can endure without repeating itself?

Movie Pairings and Activities

- Pair the film with *Heaven Can Wait* (multiple versions) for another take on second chances after death.

- Or pair it with *Truly, Madly, Deeply* (1990) for a gentler exploration of love that persists beyond loss.

- Invite viewers to imagine what they would want to carry forward into another lifetime and what they would choose to leave behind.

Final Thought

Chances Are is a lighthearted film with a surprisingly thoughtful core. It reminds us that, while love may echo across time, growth requires release. The past can be cherished without being relived, and sometimes the most meaningful second chance is the one we give ourselves in the life we are already living.

A Christmas Carol *(Multiple Film Versions, 1938-present)*

Notable Versions Include

- *A Christmas Carol* (1938) starring Reginald Owen
- *Scrooge* (1951) starring Alastair Sim
- *A Christmas Carol* (1984) starring George C. Scott
- *A Christmas Carol* (1999) starring Patrick Stewart
- *The Muppet Christmas Carol* (1992) starring Michael Caine
- *A Christmas Carol* (2009) animated, starring Jim Carrey

Based on: *A Christmas Carol* by Charles Dickens

Film Description

Charles Dickens' enduring story has been adapted for film countless times, but the core narrative remains unchanged: Ebenezer Scrooge, a miserly man emotionally frozen by fear, loss, and self-protection, is confronted by spirits who force him to reckon with his past, present, and possible future. The pivotal moment comes when the Ghost of Christmas Yet to Come shows Scrooge his own neglected grave and the indifference of a world he has failed to touch. Faced with the reality of his mortality, Scrooge chooses transformation while there is still time.

Mortality Themes

- Confrontation with one's own death
- Legacy and how we are remembered
- Social death versus physical death
- Isolation versus connection
- Redemption and second chances
- Living differently once mortality is acknowledged

Discussion Prompts

1. Why is it the vision of Scrooge's grave, rather than his past regrets, that finally prompts change?

2. How does the story distinguish between being alive and truly living?

3. What does the film suggest about the relationship between generosity, connection, and a meaningful life?

4. In what ways does Scrooge experience a kind of "death" before his transformation?

5. How do different film versions portray the Ghost of Christmas Yet to Come, and how does that affect the story's impact?

6. What parallels can be drawn between Scrooge's awakening and modern conversations about regret, burnout, or end-of-life reflection?

Movie Pairings and Activities

- Pair the movie with *It's a Wonderful Life* (1946) for another classic in which a man confronts the impact of his existence.

- Or pair it with *Defending Your Life* (1991) for a more humorous take on post-life evaluation.

- Invite participants to write a brief "future obituary" or legacy statement, then revise it on the basis of how they would want to be remembered.

Final Thought

A Christmas Carol may be wrapped in holiday tradition, but at its heart, it is one of the most effective Mortality Movies ever written. It reminds us that death clarifies what matters but transformation does not require waiting for the end. Scrooge's gift is not immortality but awareness. His story suggests that, when we live as if connection matters, we create a world that reflects that truth back to us, long before the final curtain.

City of Angels *(1998, PG-13, 1 h 54 min)*

Starring: Nicolas Cage, Meg Ryan

Directed by: Brad Silberling

Based on: *Wings of Desire* (1987) by Wim Wenders

Film Description

This romantic fantasy reimagines Wim Wenders' poetic German classic *Wings of Desire* for an American audience. Seth, an angel who quietly observes human lives in Los Angeles, falls in love with Maggie, a heart surgeon who confronts death daily in her work. Drawn to the intensity of human sensation, love, and loss, Seth makes the ultimate choice: he surrenders immortality to fully experience life. His decision brings ecstasy, vulnerability, and grief in equal measure, underscoring the fragile beauty of being human.

Mortality Themes

- Immortality versus embodied human life
- The value of pain, grief, and impermanence
- Love as a catalyst for existential choice
- Letting go after sudden loss
- Meaning found through sensory experience
- Acceptance of life's unpredictability

Discussion Prompts

1. Why does Seth choose mortality over eternal existence? What does he gain, and what does he lose?

2. How does the film portray grief as inseparable from love?

3. Maggie works daily with death as a physician. How does her relationship to mortality differ from Seth's?

4. Does the film suggest that meaning requires suffering or simply awareness?

5. How does *City of Angels* differ from traditional religious depictions of angels and the afterlife?

6. What does the ending suggest about continuing to live after profound loss?

Movie Pairings and Activities

- Pair the film with *Wings of Desire* (1987) for a deeper philosophical comparison.

- Or pair it with *Always* (1989) for another story of love that bridges life and death.

- Invite viewers to reflect on what sensory experiences make life feel the most meaningful to them and how those moments shape their values.

Final Thought

City of Angels argues that mortality is not a flaw in the human design but its defining feature. By choosing a life that can end, Seth affirms that meaning comes not from endless existence but from presence, connection, and risk. The film gently suggests that grief does not negate love's value; it proves that love mattered.

Cocoon *(1985, PG-13, 1 h 57 min)*

Starring: Don Ameche, Wilford Brimley, Hume Cronyn, Jessica Tandy, Maureen Stapleton, Gwen Verdon, Jack Gilford, Brian Dennehy

Directed by: Ron Howard

Film Description

In this warm-hearted science fiction fantasy, a group of residents at a Florida retirement community discover that swimming in a nearby pool has restored their youth, energy, and zest for life. What they do not initially realize is that the pool is infused with life-giving energy from extraterrestrials who have returned to Earth to retrieve their companions hidden underwater decades earlier. As the seniors regain vitality, they are confronted with an extraordinary choice: Remain on Earth to age and die naturally or leave the planet forever and begin a new form of existence beyond human mortality.

Mortality Themes

- Aging with dignity, humor, and companionship
- The allure of second chances and renewed vitality
- Choosing an afterlife versus accepting natural death
- Friendship and community as sources of meaning
- Legacy through relationships rather than longevity
- The emotional complexity of saying goodbye

Discussion Prompts

1. What does renewed youth represent for the characters beyond physical strength?
2. How does the film portray aging differently from more tragic depictions of old age?
3. What factors influence each character's decision to stay on Earth or leave it?
4. Is the offer of immortality portrayed as a gift, a temptation, or both?
5. How does the film suggest that connection matters more than extended life?
6. What does *Cocoon* say about fear of death versus fear of being alone?

Movie Pairings and Activities

- Pair the film with *On Golden Pond* (1981) for a grounded portrayal of aging.
- Or pair it with *The Bucket List* (2007) for another take on confronting mortality late in life.
- Invite viewers to reflect on what gives life meaning at different ages and whether more time would truly change how they live.

Final Thought

Cocoon treats mortality with kindness rather than dread. It suggests that the goal of life is not endless youth but meaningful connection. By framing afterlife as a choice rather than a certainty, the film gently reminds us that how we love, who we show up for, and how we say goodbye may matter far more than how long we live.

Cold Souls *(2009, PG-13, 1 h 41 min)*

Starring: Paul Giamatti, Emily Watson

Directed by: Sophie Barthes

Film Description

In this offbeat dramedy with fantasy elements, Paul Giamatti plays a fictionalized version of himself: an actor overwhelmed by anxiety, artistic self-doubt, and the emotional weight of performing Chekhov's *Uncle Vanya*. Searching for relief, he turns to a shadowy medical service that offers an unusual solution. They will remove his soul and place it in cryogenic storage, allowing him to function without emotional burden. What begins as a clever shortcut to peace becomes a surreal journey through loss, disconnection, and unintended consequences as Giamatti discovers that living without a soul is its own kind of suffering.

Mortality Themes

- Spiritual numbness and emotional withdrawal
- What it means to be "alive" beyond physical survival
- Identity, authenticity, and the cost of avoiding pain
- Existential anxiety and fear of meaninglessness
- The difference between relief and wholeness

Discussion Prompts

1. What does the soul represent in this film: emotion, conscience, creativity, or something else?

2. How does *Cold Souls* define being spiritually alive versus merely functioning?

3. Is Giamatti's decision an act of self-care, avoidance, or desperation?

4. How does the film use humor to explore very serious existential questions?

5. In what ways do people today try to "store away" uncomfortable feelings rather than face them?

6. Can a life without pain still be a meaningful life?

Movie Pairings and Activities

- Pair the film with *Eternal Sunshine of the Spotless Mind* (2004) to compare different approaches to emotional avoidance.

- Or pair it with *Defending Your Life* (1991) for a lighter exploration of fear, self-examination, and growth.

- Invite viewers to reflect on what parts of themselves they sometimes wish they could numb or silence, and what the cost of that disconnection might be.

Final Thought

While *Cold Souls* does not depict death directly, it wrestles deeply with existential mortality. By imagining the soul as something that can be removed, stored, or misplaced, the film asks whether emotional detachment is its own form of dying. It suggests that avoiding pain does not bring peace, only distance, and that the price of numbing ourselves may be a diminished experience of being fully alive. In a chapter devoted to imagined afterlives, *Cold Souls* offers a provocative reminder: the most fragile thing we risk losing may not be life itself, but our capacity to feel it.

The Curious Case of Benjamin Button
(2008, PG-13, 2 h 46 min)

Starring: Brad Pitt, Cate Blanchett

Directed by: David Fincher

Based on: A short story by F. Scott Fitzgerald

Film Description

This sweeping fantasy drama follows the extraordinary life of Benjamin Button who is born in 1918 with the physical body of an elderly man and ages in reverse, growing younger as the years pass. As Benjamin moves backward through the stages of life, he experiences love, loss, parenthood, war, friendship, and aging from a profoundly different vantage point. His central relationship with Daisy Williams unfolds only briefly when their physical ages align, underscoring the fleeting nature of connection. The story spans nearly a century and ends with Benjamin's death as an infant in 2003, closing a life lived entirely out of sync with time.

Mortality Themes

- The inevitability of aging and death, regardless of direction
- Timing, impermanence, and missed connections
- Love shaped and limited by mortality
- Memory, legacy, and the passage of time
- Caregiving, decline, and role reversals across the life course

Discussion Prompts

1. How does reverse aging change the way we think about the "normal" life arc?
2. Would Benjamin's life feel more meaningful, or lonelier, because of his condition?
3. What does the film suggest about the role of timing in love and relationships?
4. How does the story portray dependency, caregiving, and vulnerability at different ages?
5. If everyone ages forward but no one arrives at the same moment, what does that say about human connection?
6. What moments in the film feel the most "alive," and why?

Movie Pairings and Activities

- Pair the film with *Big Fish* (2003) for another lyrical meditation on storytelling, memory, and legacy.
- Or pair it with *Death Becomes Her* (1992) for a darkly comic counterpoint on aging and permanence.

- Invite viewers to reflect on how their understanding of time, aging, and purpose has changed across different stages of life.

Final Thought

By reversing the aging process, *The Curious Case of Benjamin Button* strips away the illusion that there is a "right" timeline for living, loving, or dying. The film reveals a deeply human truth: no matter how we move through time, we cannot escape impermanence. Benjamin's life, lived backward, teaches the same lesson as every life lived forward: that meaning is not found in perfect timing or longevity, but in presence, connection, and the willingness to love despite inevitable loss.

Death Becomes Her *(1992, PG-13, 1 h 44 min)*

Starring: Meryl Streep, Goldie Hawn, Bruce Willis, Isabella Rossellini

Directed by: Robert Zemeckis

Film Description

This dark comedy/fantasy follows two longtime rivals, actress Madeline Ashton and writer Helen Sharp, whose mutual resentment is fueled by a shared fear of aging and irrelevance. When Helen's fiancé, plastic surgeon Ernest Menville, leaves her for Madeline, the rivalry festers for years, resurfacing when the women meet again under very different circumstances.

Their lives take a surreal turn when both women encounter Lisle Von Rhuman, a glamorous and mysterious figure, who offers a potion promising eternal youth and immortality. Desperate to escape aging and reclaim control over their bodies and identities, they drink the potion expecting freedom. Instead, they find themselves trapped in a strange limbo: unable to die yet still subject to damage, decay, and constant maintenance. Their bodies require endless repair, forcing Ernest into the role of a reluctant caretaker, patching them together again and again.

Beneath the visual comedy and exaggerated performances lies a thoughtful reflection on what happens when the fear of death eclipses the joy of living. The film uses humor to explore how obsession with youth, beauty, and permanence can leave people emotionally frozen and disconnected from growth, purpose, and one another.

Mortality Themes

- The fear of aging as a stand-in for the fear of death
- Longevity versus legacy
- The body as something to manage rather than inhabit
- Identity tied to appearance and desirability
- The emotional cost of refusing to change, age, or let go
- Immortality as stagnation rather than salvation

Discussion Prompts

1. Madeline and Helen gain immortality but lose the ability to grow. What does the film suggest about the role mortality plays in shaping meaning?

2. The women are obsessed with how they look, not how they live. How does that mirror real cultural pressures around aging and beauty?

3. Ernest becomes responsible for maintaining their bodies. What parallels do you see with caregiving, medical maintenance, or end-of-life decision-making?

4. Is the potion itself the problem or the motivation behind taking it? Would immortality change us or simply amplify what is already there?

5. What does the film say about the difference between being alive and feeling alive?

6. What does the film suggest we lose when we treat aging as a defect instead of a life stage?

Movie Pairings and Activities

- Pair the movie with *Cocoon* (1985) for a gentler exploration of aging and choice.
- Pair it with *The Curious Case of Benjamin Button* (2008) for a lyrical look at time, love, and impermanence.

- Or pair it with *Defending Your Life* (1991) for humor that focuses on how we live rather than how long.

- Invite viewers to reflect on what they want to be remembered for beyond appearance or achievement.

- Ask participants what would make aging feel meaningful rather than frightening.

- Discuss where ideas about youth, beauty, and worth first took root and which ones no longer serve us.

Final Thought

Death Becomes Her makes us laugh at the absurd lengths people will go to avoid aging, but it also gently reminds us that time passing is not the enemy. Change, decline, and eventual death are what give life its texture, urgency, and meaning. The film suggests that immortality without purpose is not a gift at all and that accepting our limits may be the very thing that allows us to live more fully while we are here.

Defending Your Life *(1991, PG, 1 h 52 min)*

Starring: Albert Brooks, Meryl Streep, Rip Torn

Directed by: Albert Brooks

Film Description

After dying suddenly in a car accident, Daniel Miller finds himself in Judgment City, an afterlife way station that looks suspiciously like a pleasant, well-organized Southern California metropolis. There, the recently deceased undergo a review of their lives in a court-like process. Instead of being judged for moral sins, they are evaluated on a single criterion: how well they overcame fear during their lives.

Daniel is assigned a defense attorney and a prosecutor, and his life is examined through clips that reveal moments of courage, hesitation, avoidance, and fear-based decision-making. While preparing for his case, Daniel meets Julia, a confident and joyful woman, whose life review reveals remarkably little fear. As Daniel grows closer to her, he begins to understand how much of his own life was shaped by playing it safe.

With humor, charm, and surprising emotional depth, the film imagines an afterlife that is less about punishment or reward and more about personal growth. It gently suggests that the real work of living happens before we die and that love, courage, and risk are the central measures of a life well lived.

Mortality Themes

- Afterlife as a continuation of personal growth

- Fear as the primary obstacle to living fully

- Life review and self-reflection after death

- Accountability without condemnation

- Love as a catalyst for transformation

- The idea that courage, not perfection, is what matters

Discussion Prompts

1. In Judgment City, fear is the central measure of a life. How would your own life review look if fear were the standard?

2. Daniel avoids risk to stay safe but ends up feeling unfulfilled. Where do we see this tension in real life?

3. Julia's life is marked by openness and curiosity. What qualities does the film suggest lead to a "successful" life review?

4. How does the film's depiction of afterlife differ from the traditional religious views?

5. If you knew your life would be reviewed this way, would it change how you live now?

6. Which scenes in Daniel's 'life montage' hit you as painfully ordinary, and why do ordinary fears matter so much?

Movie Pairings and Activities

- Pair the movie with *A Matter of Life and Death* (1946) for another courtroom-style afterlife.

- Pair it with *Heaven Can Wait* (1978) for a lighter take on second chances.

- Or pair it with *The Seventh Seal* (1958) for a more somber philosophical confrontation with death.

- Invite viewers to identify fears, i.e., create a fear inventory, that have shaped major life choices.

- Ask participants to imagine what scenes might appear in their own life montage.

- Encourage choosing one small meaningful risk in the coming weeks.

Final Thought

Defending Your Life offers one of cinema's most compassionate visions of what might come after death. Instead of judgment based on rules or beliefs, it imagines an afterlife that asks a simple human question: Did you show up for your life? By wrapping that question in humor and romance, the film makes mortality feel less threatening and more motivating. It reminds us that the best way to prepare for whatever comes next may be to live with a little more courage right now.

Ghost *(1990, PG-13, 2 h 6 min)*

Starring: Patrick Swayze, Demi Moore, Whoopi Goldberg

Directed by: Jerry Zucker

Film Description

When Sam Wheat is murdered during what appears to be a random mugging, he discovers that death is not the end of his story. Trapped between worlds as a ghost, Sam watches helplessly as his partner Molly grieves his sudden loss. As he begins to understand the circumstances of his death, Sam realizes he still has unfinished business: protecting Molly, exposing his killer, and finding a way to say goodbye.

Sam's only link to the living world is Oda Mae Brown, a reluctant psychic, who discovers, to her surprise, that she can actually hear him. What begins as comic relief becomes a deeply moving partnership as Sam uses Oda Mae to communicate love, warnings, and eventually closure.

The film balances romance, suspense, humor, and fantasy, offering a vision of an afterlife where love persists, moral accountability matters, and letting go is an act of grace. And yes, the pottery wheel scene set to "Unchained Melody" remains one of the most iconic expressions of cinematic intimacy ever put on screen.

Mortality Themes

- Love that endures beyond death
- Afterlife as a place of accountability and moral reckoning
- Unfinished business and the need for closure
- Sudden death and traumatic loss
- The role of intermediaries between the living and the dead
- Letting go as the final act of love

Discussion Prompts

1. Sam remains earthbound because of unfinished business. What kinds of unfinished business do we commonly carry when someone dies suddenly?

2. The film portrays afterlife as morally structured. How does this vision compare with your own beliefs or cultural stories?

3. Oda Mae begins as a skeptic and ends as a conduit for healing. What role do storytellers, clergy, or death doulas play in real-life grief?

4. Molly's grief unfolds while Sam watches but cannot touch. How does this reflect the loneliness of grief for those left behind?

5. What helps Sam finally let go, and why does that moment feel earned?

6. How does the film distinguish between 'closure' and 'control' when someone is trying to keep a loved one safe after death?

Movie Pairings and Activities

- Pair the movie with *Truly Madly Deeply* (1990) for another ghost-love story with emotional depth.

- Pair it with *Always* (1989) for themes of love, sacrifice, and letting go.

- Or pair it with *What Dreams May Come* (1998) for a more visually elaborate afterlife vision.

- Invite viewers to discuss things left unsaid after a loss and how people find peace without resolution.

- Encourage writing a letter expressing what you hope loved ones would remember or feel after you are gone.

- Reflect on songs that connect people to loved ones who have died and why music carries memory so powerfully.

Final Thought

Ghost endures because it reassures us of something many people hope is true: that love does not end when life does. It suggests that, while death may separate bodies, it does not sever connection, responsibility, or care. At its heart, the film reminds us that the work of loving well includes knowing when to hold on and when to let go. And sometimes, the bravest goodbye is the one that sets someone free.

Ghost Town *(2008, PG-13, 1 h 42 min)*

Starring: Ricky Gervais, Greg Kinnear, Téa Leoni

Directed by: David Koepp

Film Description

Dr. Bertram Pincus is a dentist who takes pride in his spectacular dislike of people. Socially avoidant and emotionally sealed off, he prefers his patients unconscious and his personal life empty. During a routine colonoscopy, Pincus has a brief near-death experience. When he wakes up, he discovers an unexpected side effect: He can see and hear ghosts. And they will not leave him alone.

The ghosts are ordinary New Yorkers who died with unresolved business, and they quickly latch on to the one living person who can acknowledge them. Chief among them is Frank Herlihy, a charming but manipulative ghost, who pressures Pincus into helping him break up his widow's new romantic relationship. Frank promises that, if Pincus succeeds, he'll make the ghosts stop bothering him.

What unfolds is a romantic comedy with an afterlife twist where Pincus is forced into human connection, moral decision-making, and emotional growth. As he becomes involved in the lives of the living and the dead, Pincus begins to confront his own isolation, empathy, and fear of vulnerability. Beneath the humor and supernatural premise lies a gentle story about connection, accountability, and learning how to care.

Mortality Themes

- Near-death experiences as catalysts for transformation
- Ghosts as symbols of unfinished emotional business
- Accountability after death
- The consequences of emotional withdrawal while alive
- Love, regret, and letting go
- Helping the living by releasing the dead

Discussion Prompts

1. Pincus' ability to see ghosts forces him into relationships he would normally avoid. How does proximity to death change how people relate to others?

2. The ghosts are not frightening, just persistent. What real-life parallels exist for unresolved grief or unfinished business?

3. Frank wants to control events after his death. Where is the line between love, protection, and manipulation?

4. Pincus changes the most through helping others, not through getting what he wants. What does the film suggest about growth and meaning?

5. Do you see the ghosts as literal characters, metaphors, or both?

6. How does the film connect emotional isolation in life with restlessness after death?

Movie Pairings and Activities

- Pair the movie with *Ghost* (1990) for unfinished business and love beyond death.

- Pair it with *Defending Your Life* (1991) for accountability after death with humor.

- Or pair it with *The Sixth Sense* (1999) for a suspenseful, dramatic look at ghosts who need help getting their unfinished business completed.

- Invite viewers to reflect on things they would want resolved if they were suddenly gone.

- Discuss how avoidance of people can be a form of emotional self-protection.

- Ask participants to imagine what kind of ghost they would be and why.

Final Thought

Ghost Town suggests that death does not magically resolve who we are. The habits we carry in life, such as avoidance, control, generosity, or care, echo into the stories we leave behind. By turning unfinished business into persistent, awkward ghosts, the film playfully argues that the surest way to avoid becoming emotionally stuck after death is profoundly ordinary: learn to show up, take responsibility and risk connection while we are still alive.

Heaven Can Wait *(Multiple Versions)*

- *Here Comes Mr. Jordan* **(1941, Not Rated, 1 h 34 min)**

  Starring: Robert Montgomery, Claude Rains

  Directed by: Alexander Hall

- *Heaven Can Wait* **(1978, PG, 1 h 41 min)**

  Starring: Warren Beatty, Julie Christie, James Mason

  Directed by: Warren Beatty and Buck Henry

- *Down to Earth* **(2001, PG-13, 1 h 27 min)**

  Starring: Chris Rock, Regina King

  Directed by: Chris Weitz and Paul Weitz

  (Not to be confused with the 1943 Ernst Lubitsch film of the same name, listed separately below.)

Film Description

Across multiple generations, *Heaven Can Wait* has returned to the same irresistible premise: What happens when someone dies too soon because of a clerical error in the afterlife?

In each version, a man's life is cut short prematurely by an overzealous celestial employee. Realizing the mistake, Heavenly administrators scramble to correct it, only to discover the original body is no longer usable. The solution is reincarnation into another body, allowing the soul to return to Earth and finish unfinished business.

In *Here Comes Mr. Jordan*, a boxer is given a second chance to live and love. In the 1978 version, Warren Beatty plays a professional football quarterback returned to Earth in the body of a ruthless millionaire, forcing him to reconcile athletic ambition with moral awakening. *Down to Earth* updates the premise with Chris Rock as a comedian navigating race, power, and purpose after being placed into the body of a wealthy older white man.

Each retelling uses comedy and romance to explore identity, justice, and the idea that the soul exists independently from the physical body. The

Heavenly realm itself is depicted as well intentioned but imperfect, suggesting that even eternity has bureaucracy, blind spots, and learning curves.

Mortality Themes

- Death as a reversible mistake rather than a final ending
- The separation of soul and body
- Second chances and unfinished business
- Reincarnation and identity
- Moral growth through adversity
- Free will within cosmic systems

Discussion Prompts

1. What do these films suggest about the relationship between the soul and the body?
2. How does returning to life in a different body change the character's values and behavior?
3. The afterlife is portrayed as bureaucratic and fallible. Does this make death feel more approachable or less meaningful?
4. Why do second chances resonate so strongly in mortality stories?
5. Which version feels the most culturally relevant today, and why?
6. If you were granted a "clerical-error do-over," what would you do differently?

Movie Pairings and Activities

- Pair the movie with *Defending Your Life* (1991) for afterlife bureaucracy and self-examination.
- Pair it with *Chances Are* (1989) for reincarnation and love across lifetimes.
- Or pair it with *A Christmas Carol* (various versions) for moral reckoning prompted by death.
- Ask viewers what they would do differently if given one more shot at life.

- Facilitate a discussion about identity and whether personality survives physical death.

- Invite participants to imagine what they would hope an afterlife "appeals board" would say about their choices.

Final Thought

The enduring appeal of *Heaven Can Wait* lies in its reassurance that death may not end growth, learning, or love. By portraying the afterlife as imperfect but responsive, these films suggest that meaning is not fixed at the moment of death. Yet beneath the fantasy of cosmic do-overs lies a gentler challenge: live now with intention, kindness, and courage. If heaven offers second chances, perhaps life is asking us not to wait for one.

Note on a Related Film with the Same Title

Heaven Can Wait (1943, 1 h 52 min), directed by Ernst Lubitsch, tells a completely different story. In this romantic comedy, an elderly man arrives in Hades to plead his case to Satan, reviewing his life to determine whether he belongs in Hell. Witty, charming, and morally reflective, it explores life review, accountability, and the humor found in human imperfection. While unrelated in plot, it pairs beautifully with the later films as another playful meditation on judgment, memory, and meaning after death.

An Interview with God *(2018, Unrated, 1 h 37 min)*

Starring: David Strathairn, Brenton Thwaites, Yael Grobglas

Directed by: Perry Lang

Film Description

After returning from covering war zones overseas, an ambitious journalist finds himself emotionally unmoored and questioning his faith, his marriage, and the meaning of suffering he has witnessed firsthand. When he is offered the interview of a lifetime with a man who calmly claims to be God, skepticism gives way to curiosity and then to something deeper.

Over the course of several conversations, the journalist presses "God" with hard questions about pain, injustice, love, free will, and why bad things happen to good people. Rather than thunderbolts or easy answers, the exchanges are quiet, reflective, and personal. The film unfolds more like a philosophical dialogue than a traditional narrative, inviting viewers to sit with uncertainty rather than resolve it.

While *An Interview with God* received mixed critical reviews, its strength lies in its willingness to ask timeless questions without insisting on a single belief system. David Strathairn's understated performance grounds the film in warmth and humility, making the divine feel approachable rather than distant.

Mortality Themes

- Spiritual questioning after trauma and exposure to death
- Faith, doubt, and meaning in the face of suffering
- Free will and human responsibility
- The search for purpose after loss and disillusionment
- Mortality as a catalyst for spiritual inquiry

Discussion Prompts

1. Does the film require viewers to believe the man is truly God for it to be effective? Why, or why not?
2. How does the journalist's exposure to death and violence shape the questions he asks?
3. What answers, if any, does the film offer about why suffering exists?
4. How does this portrayal of God differ from the more traditional cinematic depictions?
5. Is asking questions about death, meaning and justice itself a form of faith?
6. How does the film invite viewers to sit with uncertainty rather than resolve it?

Movie Pairings and Activities

- Pair the movie with *Oh, God!* (1977) for a lighter, humorous conversation with the divine.

- Pair it with *The Shack* (2017) for grief-driven spiritual exploration.

- Or pair it with *Defending Your Life* (1991) for philosophical inquiry after death.

- Invite viewers to write down the questions they would ask if given the same opportunity.

- Facilitate conversation among viewers with different spiritual perspectives, emphasizing curiosity over debate.

- Reflect on how encounters with death have shaped personal beliefs or doubts.

Final Thought

An Interview with God suggests that mortality often leads us not to certainty but to deeper questions. Rather than offering doctrine or resolution, the film frames spiritual inquiry as a human response to witnessing suffering, loss, and death. Its quiet power lies in permission: permission to doubt, to ask, and to remain open. In the face of mortality, the film argues, connection and curiosity may matter more than definitive answers.

The Life of Chuck *(2025, R, 1 h 51 min)*

Starring: Tom Hiddleston, Mark Hamill, Chiwetel Ejiofor, Karen Gillan

Directed by: Mike Flanagan

Based on: The novella by Stephen King from *If It Bleeds*

Film Description

Told in three acts presented in a reverse chronological order, *The Life of Chuck* begins at the end of the world and slowly works backward to reveal the life of an ordinary man named Charles "Chuck" Krantz. As society unravels through natural disasters and quiet apocalyptic collapse, mysterious messages thanking Chuck for "thirty-nine great years" appear everywhere, prompting confusion about who he is and why he matters.

As the story rewinds, we encounter Chuck at different stages of his life: as a middle-aged accountant, as a grieving young man shaped by loss, and finally as a child discovering joy, rhythm, and wonder in the simplest moments. The film gently suggests that entire universes can exist within a single human mind and that even the most unremarkable lives can hold extraordinary meaning.

Rather than focusing on spectacle, *The Life of Chuck* centers on presence. It is less concerned with how the world ends than with how one person lives inside it. Mike Flanagan's adaptation honors Stephen King's meditative tone, offering a quietly profound meditation on memory, impermanence, and what it means to be fully alive.

Mortality Themes

- Life reviewed backward as a way of finding meaning
- Grief and resilience across a lifetime
- Ordinary lives as extraordinary containers of meaning
- Impermanence and the fragility of existence
- Presence, memory, and the legacy of small moments

Discussion Prompts

1. How does telling Chuck's story in reverse change your understanding of his life?
2. Why does the world seem to revolve around Chuck's death, and what might that symbolize?
3. What does the film suggest about the relationship between inner life and outer reality?
4. How does the story redefine what makes a life "important" or meaningful?
5. Which moments in Chuck's life felt the most alive to you, and why?
6. How does the film challenge the idea that legacy requires recognition or achievement?

Movie Pairings and Activities

- Pair the movie with *It's a Wonderful Life* (1946) for the impact of one life on the world.

- Pair it with *Stranger Than Fiction* (2006) for narrative awareness and mortality.

- Or pair it with *The Curious Case of Benjamin Button* (2008) for nonlinear life arcs.

- Invite viewers to sketch their own lives backward, starting from the present.

- Discuss a small ordinary moment that later revealed unexpected importance.

- Explore how being present might be an act of legacy building.

Final Thought

The Life of Chuck gently dismantles the idea that meaning depends on scale, recognition, or dramatic endings. By moving backward through an ordinary life, the film reveals how presence, attention, and small moments can hold extraordinary weight. Mortality frames the story, but it does not diminish it. Instead, the film offers a quiet reassurance: a life does not need to be loud to matter, only lived.

The Lovely Bones *(2009, PG-13, 1 h 15 min)*

Starring: Saoirse Ronan, Mark Wahlberg, Rachel Weisz, Stanley Tucci, Susan Sarandon

Directed by: Peter Jackson

Based on: The novel by Alice Sebold

Film Description

The Lovely Bones opens with an unimaginable loss: Susie Salmon, a bright and creative fourteen-year-old girl, is brutally murdered by a neighbor. Rather than following the story solely from the perspective of the living, the film places Susie in a surreal, dreamlike in-between space, somewhere between Earth and Heaven. From this liminal realm, she watches as her family, friends, and community struggle to survive the shock of her disappearance and death.

Susie's presence in this "in-between" reflects her unfinished business. She longs for justice, wrestles with anger and grief, and struggles to let go of the life she was just beginning. Meanwhile, her family fractures under the weight of the trauma: Her father becomes consumed by obsession, her mother withdraws emotionally, and her siblings process grief in very different ways.

Peter Jackson's adaptation leans into visual metaphor rather than realism, using Susie's internal landscape to explore how trauma freezes time, how grief can paralyze both the dead and the living, and how healing requires movement even when justice remains incomplete.

Mortality Themes

- Sudden, violent death and its ripple effects
- The liminal space between life and death
- Grief as emotional paralysis
- Justice versus healing
- Letting go and allowing the living to continue

Discussion Prompts

1. How does Susie's in-between world reflect her emotional state?
2. In what ways does grief manifest differently for each member of her family?
3. Does the film suggest that justice is necessary for healing or merely desired?
4. How does unresolved trauma keep both the living and the dead "stuck"?
5. What does Susie ultimately need in order to move on?
6. How does the film balance the tension between remembering the dead and allowing the living to move forward?

Movie Pairings and Activities

- Pair the movie with *Ghost* (1990) for unfinished business after death.
- Pair it with *What Dreams May Come* (1998) for visualized after-life landscapes.

- Or pair it with *Truly, Madly, Deeply* (1990) for the tension between holding on and letting go.
- Identify how different characters express grief and where it becomes immobilizing.
- Explore whether closure always requires answers.
- Invite participants to imagine what an emotional "in-between" might look like for unresolved grief.

Final Thought

The Lovely Bones does not offer easy comfort or tidy resolution. Instead, it asks a harder question: How do we live after something irreparably breaks? By placing its narrator between worlds, the film reminds us that healing is not about forgetting the dead but about learning to carry their memory without letting it stop time. Sometimes, the most loving act is allowing life to continue.

Meet Joe Black *(1998, PG-13, 2 h 58 min)*

Starring: Brad Pitt, Anthony Hopkins, Claire Forlani

Directed by: Martin Brest

Based on: *Death Takes a Holiday* (1934)

Film Description

Meet Joe Black explores an age-old question with glossy romantic sweep: What would happen if death decided to experience life as a human? When death takes corporeal form as "Joe Black," he enters the world through the life of William Parrish, a powerful media mogul approaching his sixty-fifth birthday and quietly sensing the nearness of his own death.

Joe strikes a bargain with William. In exchange for delaying his death, William will serve as Joe's guide to the human experience. As Joe observes family dinners, boardroom battles, and romantic longing, he becomes deeply entangled in the lives around him, particularly through his growing affection for William's daughter, Susan.

The film unfolds slowly and deliberately, using extended conversations and lingering scenes to explore mortality, love, legacy, and what makes life meaningful. William, knowing his time is limited, turns his attention from power and control toward integrity, connection, and preparing his loved ones for life without him.

Mortality Themes

- Death personified as a curious observer
- Conscious awareness of one's approaching death
- Legacy and ethical reckoning
- Love as both attachment and release
- Preparing for a "good death"

Discussion Prompts

1. How does Joe's perspective on humanity change as he experiences love and loss?

2. What does William Parrish do differently once he accepts that death is near?

3. Is Joe's relationship with Susan an act of love, interference, or both?

4. How does the film define a life well lived?

5. What lessons does the story offer about saying goodbye with intention?

6. How does the film distinguish between loving someone and being willing to let them go?

Movie Pairings and Activities

- Pair the movie with *Death Takes a Holiday* (1934) for the original premise.

- Pair it with *Defending Your Life* (1991) for moral reckoning after death.

- Or pair it with *The Seventh Seal* (1958) for death as a character engaging the living.

- Invite participants to consider what values or actions they would want remembered.

- Write a short letter expressing wisdom or hopes for loved ones.

- Discuss how acknowledging mortality can clarify priorities.

Final Thought

Meet Joe Black suggests that death is not the enemy of life but its clarifier. By slowing down and allowing Death to observe humanity up close, the film reminds us that meaning is found not in control or permanence but in presence, honesty, and love. When the time comes to go, what matters the most is not how long we lived but how fully we showed up while we were here.

Oh, God! *(1977, PG, 1 h 38 min)*

Starring: George Burns, John Denver, Teri Garr

Directed by: Carl Reiner

Film Description

In this light-hearted fantasy comedy, God decides it is time to check in on humanity personally. Choosing an unlikely messenger, He appears to Jerry Landers, an earnest but unassuming grocery store manager and family man. God looks exactly like a kindly older gentleman, cigar in hand, with a twinkle in his eye and a dry sense of humor.

Jerry is stunned to be chosen, especially since he is neither a religious leader nor a philosopher. God explains that this is precisely the point. Jerry represents everyday humanity, and God wants him to help spread a simple message: Take better care of one another and the planet, because life is finite and precious. As Jerry reluctantly becomes a modern-day prophet, he faces skepticism, ridicule, and legal challenges that test his faith in both God and himself.

Rather than focusing on doctrine or dogma, the film leans into practical ethics. It presents mortality not as something to fear but as the very reason compassion, responsibility, and humility matter at all.

Mortality Themes

- Finite life as the foundation of meaning
- Responsibility to future generations
- Mortality as motivation for kindness and care
- Spirituality without institutional religion
- Living well because time is limited

Discussion Prompts

1. Why does God choose an ordinary person rather than a religious authority?

2. How does the film use humor to address serious questions about life and death?

3. What does the movie suggest about human responsibility in a finite world?

4. How does acknowledging mortality change how we treat one another?

5. Is the message of the film spiritual, moral, or both?

6. How does the film suggest mortality can be a source of responsibility rather than fear?

Movie Pairings and Activities

- Pair the movie with *Bruce Almighty* (2003) for divine intervention with a comedic lens.
- Pair it with *An Interview with God* (2018) for contemporary spiritual questioning.
- Or pair it with *Defending Your Life* (1991) for moral accountability beyond death.
- Discuss what responsibilities we owe to people we will never meet.
- Identify everyday actions that reflect living well in a finite life.
- Explore how humor can make mortality discussions more approachable.

Final Thought

Oh, God! gently reminds us that mortality is not a flaw in the human design but its greatest feature. Because we do not live forever, our choices matter. Our kindness counts. Our stewardship of one another and the world carries weight. With warmth and wit, the film offers a simple truth: Living well is the most meaningful response to knowing that time is limited.

Over Her Dead Body *(2008, PG-13, 1 h 35 min)*

Starring: Eva Longoria, Paul Rudd, Lake Bell

Directed by: Jeff Lowell

Film Description

This romantic comedy fantasy begins with a spectacularly ill-timed tragedy. Kate, an over-the-top perfectionist bride, is killed on her wedding day when a falling ice sculpture ends her life just moments before she can say "I do." What follows is not her peaceful transition to the afterlife but a stubborn refusal to leave the living world behind.

Kate returns as a ghost, still deeply invested in how her life was supposed to unfold. She haunts her grieving fiancé, Henry, and becomes increasingly unhinged when he begins to form a connection with Ashley, a warm and empathetic psychic who can see and hear her. Kate's posthumous mission is simple: Sabotage the relationship and reclaim control over a life she believes should still be hers.

Beneath the slapstick humor and rom-com hijinks, the film explores how grief, attachment, and control can keep people emotionally stuck, whether they are alive or dead. It suggests that unfinished business is often less about unresolved tasks and more about unresolved acceptance.

Mortality Themes

- Unfinished business after death
- Letting go of control
- Grief as an obstacle to moving forward

- Emotional attachment versus acceptance
- The difference between love and possession

Discussion Prompts

1. What keeps Kate tethered to the living world after her death?
2. How does the film portray grief differently in the living and the dead?
3. Where is the line between love and control in Kate's behavior?
4. What does the story suggest about the necessity of letting go after loss?
5. How does humor make these themes more accessible, or does it risk minimizing them?
6. What does the film suggest about how expectations around "how life should have gone" can complicate grief?

Movie Pairings and Activities

- Pair the movie with *Ghost* (1990) for a more earnest take on unfinished business.
- Pair it with *Truly, Madly, Deeply* (1990) for love complicated by lingering spirits.
- Or pair it with *Ghost Town* (2008), a comedy with more ghosts who have unfinished business.
- Invite participants to reflect on something they are holding on to that may no longer serve them.
- Discuss whether Kate's actions are driven more by grief or ego.
- Imagine alternative afterlife rules that might help characters release control.

Final Thought

Over Her Dead Body uses broad comedy to explore a surprisingly familiar truth: Letting go can be harder than dying. The film reminds us that clinging to how things "should have been" can trap both the living and the dead. In the end, peace comes not from control but from acceptance, a lesson that resonates long after the laughter fades.

The Shack *(2017, PG-13, 2 h 12 min)*

Starring: Sam Worthington, Octavia Spencer, Tim McGraw, Radha Mitchell

Directed by: Stuart Hazeldine

Film Description

After the brutal abduction and murder of his young daughter, Mack Phillips is left shattered by grief, guilt, and rage. Years later, he receives a mysterious letter inviting him back to the remote shack where evidence of his daughter's death was discovered. Expecting danger or cruelty, Mack instead encounters a startling and unconventional vision of God, along with manifestations of Jesus and the Holy Spirit.

Over the course of a weekend, Mack is drawn into intense conversations about suffering, love, forgiveness, justice, and the nature of God. The shack becomes a liminal space, somewhere between the physical world and the spiritual realm, where Mack confronts the pain he has buried and the questions that haunt him the most. Rather than offering easy answers, the film invites viewers into the messy, uncomfortable work of grappling with loss and meaning after tragedy.

Based on the best-selling novel by William P. Young, *The Shack* blends grief drama with spiritual fantasy, presenting the afterlife not as a fixed destination but as a relational experience shaped by love, compassion, and choice.

Mortality Themes

- Grief after the death of a child
- Guilt and the burden of unanswered questions
- Forgiveness as a path to healing
- Theodicy: why suffering exists
- Continuing bonds with the dead
- Spiritual encounters as part of grief processing

Discussion Prompts

1. How does Mack's grief shape the way he experiences God and the afterlife?

2. The film suggests that forgiveness is more for the living than the dead. Do you agree?

3. How does *The Shack* portray God differently from traditional depictions, and how does that affect its message?

4. What role does guilt play in Mack's inability to heal?

5. Does the film offer comfort, challenge, or both to people who are grieving?

6. How does the film portray the difference between understanding suffering intellectually and processing it emotionally?

Movie Pairings and Activities

- Pair the film with *An Interview with God* (2018) for conversations about faith and doubt.

- Pair it with *What Dreams May Come* (1998) for love and loss across spiritual realms.

- Or pair the film with *Rabbit Hole* (2010) for a non-fantasy exploration of parental grief.

- Invite viewers to name the questions about life and death they find the hardest to answer.

- Discuss situations where forgiveness feels impossible and what might make it achievable.

- Explore how different cultures imagine encounters with the divine after loss.

Final Thought

The Shack does not pretend to solve grief or explain suffering away. Instead, it offers a gentle, if sometimes provocative, invitation to sit with pain and ask hard questions in the presence of love. Whether viewers see it as theology, metaphor, or grief fantasy, the film reminds us that healing often begins not with answers but with the courage to return to the places we fear the most.

The Sixth Sense *(1999, PG-13, 1 h 47 min)*

Starring: Bruce Willis, Haley Joel Osment, Toni Collette

Written and Directed by: M. Night Shyamalan

Film Description

Dr. Malcolm Crowe is a respected child psychologist trying to recover professionally and personally after a former patient violently confronts him. He soon begins working with Cole Sear, a quiet, anxious young boy, who confesses a terrifying secret: He can see dead people. These spirits appear as they were at the moment of their deaths, unaware that they are no longer alive, and many are desperate to be heard.

As Malcolm attempts to help Cole cope with his gift, the film unfolds as both a psychological thriller and a deeply emotional story about fear, trust, and healing. Cole's journey is not about banishing the dead but learning how to listen to them. Meanwhile, Malcolm struggles with his own sense of purpose and connection, unaware that his understanding of life, death, and himself is incomplete.

The film's now-famous twist reframes the entire story, transforming what first appears to be a ghost tale into a meditation on denial, unfinished business, and the quiet work of acceptance. At its heart, *The Sixth Sense* is not about being haunted by the dead but about learning how to live with truth.

Mortality Themes

- Fear of death versus acceptance of death
- Unfinished business and unresolved relationships
- Denial of one's own death
- Communication between the living and the dead
- Grief, trauma, and emotional isolation
- Healing through listening and acknowledgment

Discussion Prompts

1. The ghosts in the film do not know they are dead. What might this suggest about denial and unfinished business?

2. Cole learns that helping the dead means listening rather than fixing. How does this apply to supporting the grieving?

3. How does Malcolm's journey mirror the experiences of the ghosts he encounters?

4. What role does storytelling play in making sense of fear and loss in the film?

5. How does the film's twist change your understanding of grief and connection?

6. How does the film suggest that acceptance, rather than explanation, is what allows both the living and the dead to find peace?

Movie Pairings and Activities

- Pair the movie with *Ghost* (1990) for unfinished business and love beyond death.

- Pair it with *The Others* (2001) for denial and haunting as a metaphor.

- Or pair it with *Truly, Madly, Deeply* (1990) for continuing bonds with the dead.

- Invite participants to reflect on what they would want said or resolved if time were limited.

- Discuss how being heard can be more healing than being reassured.

- Explore how fear of death shifts when it is approached with understanding rather than avoidance.

Final Thought

The Sixth Sense endures not because of its twist but because of its tenderness. It reminds us that what frightens us the most about death is often what remains unsaid or unresolved. By learning to listen to the dead, the living find their way forward. In that sense, the film suggests that acceptance is not an ending but a quiet beginning.

Stranger Than Fiction *(2006, PG-13, 1 h 53 min)*

Starring: Will Ferrell, Emma Thompson, Maggie Gyllenhaal, Dustin Hoffman

Directed by: Marc Forster

Film Description

Harold Crick is a meticulous solitary IRS auditor whose life runs on routines, numbers, and predictability. One morning, he begins hearing a calm, omniscient narrator describing his every move, including his thoughts and habits. At first, Harold fears he is losing his mind. Then the narration ominously declares that his death is imminent.

Harold soon discovers the unthinkable: He is a fictional character in a novel being written by Karen Eiffel, an acclaimed author famous for killing off her protagonists. Faced with the certainty of his own narrative death, Harold is forced to confront a question he has long avoided: How should one live when time is limited?

What follows is not a frantic attempt to escape death but a quiet transformation. Harold learns to embrace risk, connection, joy, and love. He begins to live deliberately, choosing meaning over safety. Through its whimsical premise, *Stranger Than Fiction* becomes a gentle meditation on mortality, authorship, and the power of choice.

Mortality Themes

- Awareness of death as a catalyst for meaningful living
- Existential anxiety and personal agency
- The tension between fate and free will
- Regret, missed opportunities, and second chances
- Choosing connection, love, and purpose

Discussion Prompts

1. How does Harold's awareness of his impending death change the way he lives?

2. In what ways do people live as if their lives are already written for them?

3. What does the film suggest about free will versus fate?

4. How does humor soften the film's exploration of mortality?

5. If you knew your story's ending, what chapters would you rewrite now?

6. What does the film suggest about who, or what, gets to be the "author" of a meaningful life?

Movie Pairings and Activities

- Pair the movie with *About Time* (2013) for mortality and intentional living.

- Pair it with *Ikiru* (1952) for legacy and purpose at the end of life.

- Or pair it with *The Bucket List* (2007) for death as a wake-up call.

- Invite viewers to name the current "chapter" of their lives and what they hope comes next.

- Reflect on one small change that would make daily life feel more meaningful.

- Explore what makes life feel "well written."

Final Thought

Stranger Than Fiction reminds us that mortality is not merely an ending but an editor. Knowing that our time is finite sharpens the choices we make and clarifies what matters the most. The film gently suggests that a life doesn't need to be long or extraordinary to be meaningful. It simply needs to be lived on purpose.

What Dreams May Come *(1998, PG-13, 1 h 53 min)*

Starring: Robin Williams, Annabella Sciorra, Cuba Gooding Jr., Max von Sydow

Directed by: Vincent Ward

Film Description

After dying in a car accident, pediatrician Chris Nielsen awakens in an afterlife unlike anything he imagined. His heaven is a living painting shaped by color, memory, and love, reflecting the artistic soul of his wife Annie. Chris slowly learns how this world works, guided by familiar spirits who help him understand that the afterlife is deeply personal, formed by one's inner life.

Tragedy deepens when Annie, devastated by grief, dies by suicide and descends into a hell shaped by despair and isolation. Refusing to accept eternal separation, Chris sets out on a dangerous journey to find her, even if it means losing himself. The film becomes less about spectacle and more about devotion: the belief that love can cross any boundary, including death itself.

Visually lush and emotionally ambitious, *What Dreams May Come* offers a bold, unconventional vision of the afterlife while exploring grief, guilt, and the human longing for reunion.

Mortality Themes

- Afterlife as a reflection of inner emotional states
- Grief, suicide, and survivor guilt
- Love as a force that transcends death
- The impact of unresolved pain on both the living and the dead
- Healing, forgiveness, and redemption beyond the grave

Discussion Prompts

1. How does the film's depiction of heaven and hell differ from traditional religious portrayals?
2. What does the movie suggest about the relationship between mental health and afterlife?

3. How is grief shown as both a living and post-death experience?

4. Is Chris' journey an act of love, denial, or both?

5. How does the film handle the tension between free will and fate after death?

6. How does the film explore the difference between rescuing someone you love and allowing them to find their own way toward healing?

Movie Pairings and Activities

- Pair the movie with *Truly, Madly, Deeply* (1990) for love continuing after death.

- Pair it with *Ghost* (1990) for unfinished business and devotion.

- Or pair it with *After Life* (1998, Japan) for personal visions of the afterlife.

- Invite viewers to imagine what their own heaven might look like and why.

- Talk openly about how grief can isolate people and what helps reconnect them.

- Encourage drawing or writing inspired by the film's visual style as a way to process emotion.

Final Thought

What Dreams May Come dares to imagine that the afterlife is not a fixed destination but a landscape shaped by love, memory, and pain. While its ideas may not align with every belief system, the film offers a powerful truth: Grief does not end with death, and neither does love. In its most hopeful moments, it suggests that compassion, connection, and courage remain possible even beyond the final goodbye.

It's a Wonderful Life *(1946, PG, 2 h 10 min)*

Starring: James Stewart, Donna Reed, Lionel Barrymore

Directed by: Frank Capra

Film Description

On Christmas Eve in the small town of Bedford Falls, businessman George Bailey finds himself overwhelmed by financial ruin, crushing responsibility, and a lifetime of postponed dreams. Feeling trapped and believing his family and community would be better off without him, George contemplates suicide. In response, Heaven intervenes.

Clarence, a gentle and earnest guardian angel trying to earn his wings, is sent to show George what the world would look like had he never been born. As George moves through a parallel version of his town, he witnesses the ripple effects of his absence: lives diminished, kindness undone, and a community hollowed out by loss. What George learns is not that his life was perfect but that it mattered deeply.

Often remembered as a holiday classic, *It's a Wonderful Life* is ultimately a profound meditation on despair, meaning, and the unseen impact one person can have simply by showing up for others.

Mortality Themes

- Suicidal ideation and crisis of meaning
- The value of a single life and cumulative impact
- Legacy through everyday acts of kindness
- Community as a protective factor against despair
- Redemption, gratitude, and renewed purpose

Discussion Prompts

1. What finally shifts George's desire to die into a desire to live?
2. How does the film redefine success and failure?
3. What does Clarence's intervention say about how we measure a "good life"?

4. In what ways do small ordinary actions create a lasting legacy?

5. How might this story resonate differently for viewers at various life stages?

6. How does the film challenge the idea that a life's value is only visible during moments of success or recognition?

Movie Pairings and Activities

- Pair the movie with *Stranger Than Fiction* (2006) for awareness of mortality prompting life changes.

- Pair it with *A Man Called Otto* (2022) for grief, despair, and reconnection.

- Or pair it with *The Family Man* (2000) for alternate-life reflections.

- Invite participants to reflect on how their presence has shaped others' lives.

- Write a letter (sent or unsent) acknowledging someone whose quiet actions mattered.

- Discuss how connection can act as prevention during times of despair.

Final Thought

It's a Wonderful Life reminds us that legacy is rarely built through grand gestures. It is shaped by showing up, offering help, and staying when it would be easier to walk away. The film gently argues that, even when life feels unbearable, our absence would leave a void we cannot see from inside our pain. Sometimes the greatest gift is simply being here.

Death Fantasy and Afterlife Visions: Closing Thoughts

After spending time with these cinematic visions of what lies beyond, one thing becomes clear: Stories of the afterlife aren't really about the dead at all. They're about us as the living, struggling to make sense of impermanence, longing, love, fear, and meaning.

Fantasy gives us emotional language when real life feels too sharp. It offers metaphors big enough to hold our hopes, our regrets, and our wild imaginings. These films help us articulate what we can't always say plainly: that we want love to endure, we want justice for those taken too soon, we want forgiveness, we want connection, and we want reassurance that our stories don't end abruptly at the final breath.

Whether the afterlife is shown as a shimmering landscape, a bustling bureaucracy, a romantic detour, or a comic misadventure, the message underneath is surprisingly grounded: What we do in life echoes into whatever comes next. And how we love shapes how we are remembered.

Fantasy may give death special effects, but the feelings are always real. When you step back from these films, walk away with curiosity, comfort, and openness. Give yourself the courage to live more fully before the credits roll.

GRIEF AND GROWTH

Introduction

Grief is not a problem to be solved. It is an experience to be lived. The films in this chapter explore what happens after the funeral, after the casseroles stop arriving, and after the world quietly expects life to return to "normal." These stories sit with loss in all its forms, sudden and anticipated, public and private, complicated and unresolved. They show grief not as a straight line but as a winding path shaped by love, memory, anger, guilt, and resilience.

What unites these films is their honesty. They do not rush healing or promise tidy endings. Instead, they show how grief reshapes identity, relationships, and purpose. Some characters fall apart. Others are quietly transformed. Many do both. Through humor, sorrow, conflict, and connection, these stories remind us that grief is not the opposite of love; it is the evidence of it.

Movies offer us a rare gift. They let us witness grief from the inside while sitting safely on the outside. In doing so, they give language to feelings that are often difficult to express and the permission to grieve in our own imperfect ways.

Bonneville *(2006, PG, 1 h 33 min)*

Starring: Jessica Lange, Kathy Bates, Joan Allen

Directed by: Christopher N. Rowley

Film Description

When Arvilla's husband, Joe, dies while they are traveling abroad, she makes the practical decision to have his body cremated so she can bring him home. What should be a straightforward act of care quickly becomes complicated. As Joe's second wife, Arvilla discovers that his adult daughter holds certain legal rights that were never updated with a new will. Suddenly, grief is tangled with paperwork, family dynamics, and unfinished business.

Rather than staying stuck, Arvilla embarks on an ash-scattering road trip with two longtime friends. Their journey across the American West becomes less about geography and more about transformation. Along the way, the women confront loss, aging, friendship, regret, and the quiet courage it takes to keep living after love ends. *Bonneville* is gentle, reflective, and grounded in the small truths that emerge when grief is shared rather than carried alone.

Mortality Themes

- Grief as a process, not a problem to be solved
- Honoring final wishes and the complications of blended families
- Cremation and ash scattering as ritual and release
- Friendship as a container for mourning
- Personal transformation after loss
- The intersection of love, legality, and legacy

Discussion Prompts

1. Arvilla's grief unfolds slowly and quietly. How does this depiction differ from more dramatic portrayals of loss?

2. What role do Arvilla's friends play in her healing? How does companionship change the experience of mourning?

3. How does the lack of updated estate planning complicate Joe's death? What emotions arise when legal realities collide with personal relationships?

4. Ash scattering becomes a central ritual in the film. What makes a ritual meaningful even when it doesn't go as planned?

5. Each woman on the trip is carrying her own losses. How does shared grief open space for honesty and growth?

6. How does the journey help Arvilla shift from honoring Joe's death to reclaiming her own life, and what signals that growth without erasing grief?

Movie Pairings and Activities

- Pair the movie with *Elizabethtown* (2005), *Smoke Signals* (1998), *Around the Bend* (2004) or *About Schmidt* (2002) for road-trip reflections shaped by death.

- Invite participants to reflect on what they would want done with their remains and why. Follow with a discussion about how those wishes could be clearly communicated and legally protected.

- Have viewers write a short "travel map" of their own grief journey: where they've been, where they feel stuck, and where they hope to go next.

Final Thought

Bonneville reminds us that grief does not demand grand gestures. Sometimes healing arrives quietly, in the passenger seat of a long drive, in shared laughter, or in the simple act of letting go. The film honors the truth that love does not end when life does and that moving forward does not mean leaving the dead behind but learning how to carry them differently.

Calendar Girls *(2003, PG-13, 1 h 48 min)*

Starring: Helen Mirren, Julie Walters, Annette Crosbie, Celia Imrie, Penelope Wilton

Directed by: Nigel Cole

Film Description

Chris and Annie are longtime friends and members of a women's charitable organization in a small English town. After Annie's husband dies of leukemia, she is frustrated by the bleak hospital waiting room where families sit during long hours of uncertainty. Wanting to honor her husband's memory in a tangible way, she proposes an unconventional fundraiser. With the support of their close-knit group of friends, the women create a tasteful nude calendar that celebrates humor, friendship, and the realities of aging bodies. Based on true life events, what begins as a deeply personal act of remembrance becomes a public statement about resilience, visibility, and living fully after loss.

Mortality Themes

- Grief as a catalyst for purpose
- Honoring the dead through meaningful action
- Aging, identity, and changing bodies
- Friendship and community as sources of resilience
- Transformation after loss
- Legacy created through service

Discussion Prompts

1. How does Annie's grief influence her desire to take action rather than remain quiet or reserved?

2. In what ways does friendship support the women as they navigate loss and vulnerability?

3. How does the film challenge cultural assumptions about aging, especially for women?

4. What makes this fundraiser both a memorial and a form of healing?

5. How can acts of remembrance evolve into something larger than originally intended?

6. How does public visibility, such as being seen, photographed, and talked about, change the women's relationship to both grief and self-worth?

Movie Pairings and Activities

- Pair the movie with *Steel Magnolias* (1989) or *Boys on the Side* (1995) to explore female friendships, illness, and loss.

- Invite viewers to reflect on ways they might honor a loved one through service or creativity.

- Discuss how community-based memorials differ from private expressions of grief.

Final Thought

Calendar Girls shows that grief does not always arrive quietly or stay hidden. Sometimes it inspires laughter, courage, and unexpected reinvention. The film gently reminds us that honoring the dead can be joyful, communal, and even a little daring and that growth often begins when we allow ourselves to be seen.

Captain Fantastic *(2016, R, 1 h 58 min)*

Starring: Viggo Mortensen, George MacKay, Samantha Isler, Annalise Basso

Directed by: Matt Ross

Film Description

Ben Cash is raising his six children far from mainstream society in the forests of the Pacific Northwest, teaching them survival skills, critical thinking, and radical self-reliance. Their mother, Leslie, is away receiving treatment for severe mental illness. When news arrives that Leslie has died by suicide, the family is thrust into grief and forced to leave their isolated world to attend her funeral. Leslie's final wishes challenge both legal norms and family expectations, setting up a collision between Ben's values, the children's emotional needs, and the demands of extended family and society. The journey becomes both a literal road trip and an emotional reckoning with loss, responsibility, and the limits of idealism.

Mortality Themes

- Suicide and its impact on surviving family members
- Children confronting death and grief
- Autonomy in death planning versus legal and cultural constraints
- Grief complicated by mental illness
- Parenting through loss
- Balancing ideals with emotional reality

Discussion Prompts

1. How do Ben's parenting choices shape the children's understanding of death and grief?

2. What tensions arise between honoring Leslie's wishes and protecting the children?

3. How does the film portray the long shadow of mental illness after death?

4. In what ways does grief expose cracks in Ben's philosophy of self-sufficiency?

5. How do societal norms around funerals and death clash with the family's values?

6. How does the film suggest grief requires flexibility rather than ideological purity, especially when children are involved?

Movie Pairings and Activities

- Pair the movie with *Ordinary People* (1980) or *Rabbit Hole* (2010) to explore family responses to suicide.
- Discuss how children of different ages process loss differently.
- Invite reflection on how far personal wishes should go when others are left behind.

Final Thought

Captain Fantastic reminds us that grief does not exist in a vacuum; it intersects with culture, law, parenting, and mental health. The film does not offer easy answers, but it asks essential questions about how we honor the dead while caring for the living, especially when loss disrupts the ideals we thought could sustain us.

The Cemetery Club *(1993, PG-13, 1 h 46 min)*

Starring: Ellen Burstyn, Olympia Dukakis, Diane Ladd

Directed by: Bill Duke

Film Description

Three longtime friends, all widows, meet regularly at the cemetery where their husbands are buried. Their shared ritual keeps them connected, but each woman is moving through grief in her own way. Esther cautiously allows herself to consider companionship again. Doris clings tightly to tradition, memory, and the life she knew. Lucille plunges enthusiastically back into dating, determined to prove she is still alive, desirable, and relevant. As their paths begin to diverge, the women are forced to confront difficult questions about loyalty, identity, and whether loving again means letting go of the past.

Mortality Themes

- Widowhood and long-term grief
- Continuing bonds with the dead
- Redefining identity after the death of a partner
- Loneliness and companionship in later life
- Guilt and permission to love again
- Friendship as a container for grief

Discussion Prompts

1. How do Esther, Doris, and Lucille each represent different grief styles?

2. What role does the cemetery play in maintaining connection to the past?

3. Why does moving forward feel like a betrayal for some characters?

4. How does aging complicate conversations about love, desire, and loss?

5. What does the film suggest about friendship as a lifeline during grief?

6. What does the film suggest about giving ourselves permission to change after loss, even when others expect us to stay the same?

Movie Pairings and Activities

- Pair the movie with *Hope Springs* (2012) or *Book Club* (2018) to discuss aging, intimacy, and reinvention.

- Invite participants to reflect on rituals that help them stay connected to loved ones who have died.

- Discuss how grief changes over time rather than disappearing.

Final Thought

The Cemetery Club offers a compassionate look at how grief reshapes identity long after the funeral is over. It reminds us that there is no single timeline for mourning, no universal rule for when it is acceptable to move forward, and no expiration date on the need for love, connection, and meaning.

Good Grief *(2023, R, 1 h 40 min)*

Starring: Dan Levy, Ruth Negga, Himesh Patel, Luke Evans, Celia Imrie

Directed by: Dan Levy

Film Description

Marc is reeling after the sudden death of his husband, Oliver, during a holiday gathering. Nearly a year into mourning, Marc uncovers a painful truth: Oliver had been unfaithful and secretly maintained an apartment in Paris. Shaken by grief layered with betrayal, Marc's closest friends, Sophie and Thomas, insist on whisking him away to Paris. What begins as an escape becomes a reckoning as Marc confronts unresolved love, anger, longing, and the complicated reality of loving someone who was not who he believed them to be. The film blends dark humor, emotional vulnerability, and an LGBTQ+ perspective on grief, friendship, and rebuilding a sense of self.

Mortality Themes

- Sudden death and unresolved grief
- Grief complicated by betrayal and secrecy
- Identity loss after the death of a partner
- Continuing bonds that include anger and disappointment
- Friendship as a stabilizing force during mourning
- Reconstructing meaning after emotional rupture

Discussion Prompts

1. How does discovering Oliver's secret change Marc's grief process?
2. Can grief coexist with anger, betrayal, and love at the same time?
3. What role do Sophie and Thomas play in Marc's healing?
4. How do location and travel function as catalysts for emotional movement?
5. In what ways does the film challenge idealized narratives about the dead?
6. How does accepting a more complex truth about Oliver allow Marc to begin forming a more honest sense of self after loss?

Movie Pairings and Activities

- Pair the movie with *Rabbit Hole* (2010) or *Manchester by the Sea* (2016) to explore unresolved grief.
- Invite viewers to reflect on how new information after a death can reshape memory.
- Discuss how humor can function as both protection and release in mourning.

Final Thought

Good Grief reminds us that mourning is rarely tidy, especially when love is complicated by secrets. It offers permission to grieve not only who someone was but who we thought they were and to recognize that healing often begins when we allow the full truth of our loss to surface.

Gravity *(2013, PG-13, 1 h 31 min)*

Starring: Sandra Bullock, George Clooney

Directed by: Alfonso Cuarón

Film Description

Dr. Ryan Stone is a brilliant medical engineer on her first space mission, still quietly shattered by the accidental death of her young daughter back on Earth. When a routine spacewalk turns catastrophic, leaving her adrift in the vast silence of space, survival becomes both a physical and emotional challenge. Veteran astronaut Matt Kowalski offers guidance, humor, and calm in the face of disaster, helping Ryan navigate impossible odds. As oxygen dwindles and hope flickers, Ryan confronts her grief, her desire to give up, and her instinct to keep going. The journey back to Earth becomes a powerful metaphor for rebirth, resilience, and choosing life after devastating loss.

Mortality Themes

- Grief following the death of a child
- Isolation and existential fear
- Near-death experiences and survival instinct
- Letting go of the dead while honoring their impact
- Rebirth and renewal after trauma
- Choosing life in the aftermath of loss

Discussion Prompts

1. How does Ryan's grief shape her response to crisis and survival?
2. In what ways does space function as a metaphor for emotional isolation?

3. What role does Matt Kowalski play in Ryan's psychological journey, beyond practical help?

4. How does the film portray the moment when someone decides to keep living?

5. What does Ryan's return to Earth symbolize in terms of growth after grief?

6. How does the film suggest that survival after loss is not just about endurance, but about reclaiming meaning and connection?

Movie Pairings and Activities

- Pair the film with *Wild* (2014) or *Cast Away* (2000) to explore survival as emotional transformation.

- Invite viewers to discuss moments when grief made life feel unbearable.

- Use the film as a prompt to talk about how loss can disconnect us from meaning and how reconnection begins.

Final Thought

Gravity shows that grief can leave us untethered, gasping for air in a world that no longer feels safe. Yet it also reminds us that, even after unbearable loss, the human instinct to survive, adapt, and begin again can carry us home.

Hamnet *(2025, PG-13, 2 h 5 min)*

Starring: Jessie Buckley, Paul Mescal

Directed by: Chloé Zhao

Film Description

Set in sixteenth-century England, *Hamnet* follows Agnes and William Shakespeare after the death of their eleven-year-old son from the plague. Agnes, a healer deeply attuned to the natural world, remains rooted in home and family, tending to her surviving children while carrying a grief that is private, physical, and consuming. William, often absent and emotionally distant, turns to language and storytelling to make sense of the loss. Over time, his sorrow finds expression in a play that will outlive them both. Rather than focusing on literary legacy, the film centers on the intimate fractured experience of parental grief and the very different ways two people mourn the same child.

Mortality Themes

- Parental grief after the death of a child
- Sudden death from illness and historical vulnerability
- Gendered expressions of mourning
- Creative expression as a response to loss
- Continuing bonds with the dead
- Transformation of grief into meaning and legacy

Discussion Prompts

1. How do Agnes and William grieve differently, and why do those differences create distance between them?
2. What role does Agnes' identity as a healer play in how she understands death and loss?
3. How does the historical setting shape the characters' relationship with mortality?
4. In what ways does storytelling become both an escape from grief and a container for it?
5. How does the film portray the idea of legacy when the loss feels unbearably personal?
6. How does the film challenge the idea that shared grief naturally brings people closer together?

Movie Pairings and Activities

- Pair the film with *Rabbit Hole* (2010) or *Ordinary People* (1980) to compare portrayals of parental grief.
- Discuss how creativity, ritual, or work has helped people process loss in their own lives.

- Invite viewers to reflect on how grief changes relationships, even loving ones.

Final Thought

Hamnet reminds us that grief does not resolve neatly and it does not look the same from one heart to another. It shows how love endures not by erasing loss but by carrying it forward, sometimes quietly, sometimes through art, and always with tenderness for what was deeply cherished.

The Hours *(2002, PG-13, 1 h 50 min)*

Starring: Nicole Kidman, Julianne Moore, Meryl Streep

Directed by: Stephen Daldry

Film Description

The Hours weaves together the lives of three women across three different eras, each bound by Virginia Woolf's novel *Mrs. Dalloway* and by the weight of mortality pressing in on ordinary days. In the 1920s, Virginia Woolf struggles with severe mental illness while writing the novel that anchors the film. In the 1950s, Laura Brown, a suburban housewife, feels trapped by conformity and quietly contemplates escape from her life and from life itself. In the early 2000s, Clarissa Vaughan cares for her longtime friend Richard, who is dying of AIDS, while facing anticipatory grief and questions about the choices that shaped her own life. The film's title reflects the fragile hours in which decisions are made, lives pivot, and meaning is negotiated moment by moment.

Mortality Themes

- Suicide and suicidal ideation
- Living with chronic mental illness
- Anticipatory grief and caregiving
- Illness and dying during the AIDS crisis
- The weight of everyday choices
- Meaning, regret, and legacy

- How art and literature connect lives across time

Discussion Prompts

1. How do the three women experience despair differently, and what shapes their responses to it?

2. In what ways does caregiving become both an act of love and a source of grief for Clarissa?

3. How does the film portray suicide without romanticizing it?

4. What does the story suggest about the cumulative impact of small everyday decisions?

5. How does *Mrs. Dalloway* function as both a mirror and a lifeline for the characters?

6. Which character's relationship to mortality felt the most relatable to you, and why?

Movie Pairings and Activities

- Pair the movie with *Still Alice* (2014) to explore identity, illness, and loss of self.

- Or pair it with *Angels in America* (2003 TV miniseries) to deepen conversations about AIDS-era grief and caregiving.

- Invite viewers to reflect on moments when a single day or decision altered the direction of their lives.

Final Thought

The Hours reminds us that mortality is not only present at the moment of death but woven into the fabric of daily living. It honors the quiet courage required to endure, to care, and to choose life again and again even when the weight of grief makes every hour feel heavy.

Last Tango in Paris *(1972, NC-17, 2 h 9 min)*

Starring: Marlon Brando, Maria Schneider

Directed by: Bernardo Bertolucci

Film Description

Often remembered for its controversial sexuality, *Last Tango in Paris* is, at its core, a raw and an unsettling portrait of unresolved grief. Paul, a middle-aged American living in Paris, is consumed by the recent suicide of his wife. In his emotional numbness and rage, he enters a deliberately anonymous sexual relationship with a young woman, Jeanne. The relationship is built on avoidance rather than intimacy, with Paul refusing names, history, or emotional connection.

As the film unfolds, it becomes clear that the sexual intensity is less about desire and more about Paul's attempt to escape the unbearable weight of loss. In one of the film's most harrowing scenes, he speaks directly to his dead wife's body, unleashing fury, guilt, and despair that had previously been displaced into the relationship. The film offers an unflinching look at grief that has no container, ritual, or support system.

Mortality Themes

- Complicated grief following suicide
- Disenfranchised mourning and emotional isolation
- Grief expressed through anger, avoidance, and risk taking
- The absence of ritual or support after loss
- Destructive coping mechanisms in bereavement

Discussion Prompts

1. How does Paul's grief shape his behavior and relationships throughout the film?

2. In what ways does the absence of mourning rituals contribute to his emotional unraveling?

3. How does the film challenge or reinforce cultural ideas about how grief should look?

4. What happens when grief is expressed without boundaries or accountability?

5. Can avoidance of emotional truth ever serve as a temporary survival strategy, or does it inevitably deepen suffering?

6. What responsibility, if any, do communities or cultures have to provide structure for grief when individuals cannot find it themselves?

Movie Pairings and Activities

- Pair the film with *Manchester by the Sea* (2016) for a comparison of contained versus explosive grief.

- Or pair it with *A Single Man* (2009) to explore different responses to partner loss and emotional isolation.

- Invite viewers to reflect on how grief shows up physically, behaviorally, or relationally when it has nowhere else to go.

- Discuss the role of ritual, therapy, or community in providing safer outlets for mourning.

Final Thought

Last Tango in Paris is not a comforting film, nor does it offer redemption or a tidy resolution. What it does offer is a stark warning about what can happen when grief is denied voice, witness, and structure. Mourning does not disappear when ignored. It finds expression elsewhere, sometimes in ways that harm both the griever and those around them. This film reminds us that grief demands acknowledgment, and when it is not given space to breathe, it can consume everything in its path.

Love Story *(1970, PG, 1 h 40 min)*

Starring: Ali MacGraw, Ryan O'Neal

Directed by: Arthur Hiller

Film Description

Love Story is a deceptively simple romantic drama that becomes a meditation on loss, helplessness, and anticipatory grief. Oliver Barrett IV, a wealthy

Harvard student, falls in love with Jenny Cavilleri, a sharp working-class Radcliffe student. Their relationship unfolds against family conflict, class differences, and youthful idealism.

Midway through the film, the tone shifts when Jenny is diagnosed with a terminal illness. The couple is forced to confront mortality far sooner than expected. Despite love, intelligence, and financial resources, they discover there are limits to control and fairness in life. The film captures the quiet devastation of watching someone you love decline, as well as the emotional isolation that can come with anticipatory grief.

The story became iconic for its emotional restraint and cultural impact, including the much-quoted line, "Love means never having to say you're sorry," a sentiment that continues to spark debate about vulnerability, accountability, and emotional expression in relationships.

Mortality Themes

- Anticipatory grief in young adulthood
- Illness disrupting life narratives and future plans
- Powerlessness in the face of terminal diagnosis
- Love under the shadow of impending loss
- Family estrangement and reconciliation through grief

Discussion Prompts

1. How does anticipatory grief shape Oliver's behavior before and after Jenny's diagnosis?

2. What does the film suggest about control, privilege, and fairness in the face of illness?

3. How does the couple's youth affect how they experience and express grief?

4. What do you make of the line "Love means never having to say you're sorry"? Does it hold up?

5. How does this film compare to the more modern portrayals of illness and dying?

6. How does anticipatory grief alter the way love is expressed compared to grief after death?

Movie Pairings and Activities

- Pair the movie with *The Fault in Our Stars* (2014) to explore generational shifts in how young people face terminal illness.

- Or pair it with *Brian's Song* (1971) for another look at youth, illness, and emotional restraint.

- Invite viewers to reflect on how anticipatory grief differs from grief after death.

- Discuss how families respond differently when illness enters the picture.

Final Thought

Love Story endures not because it is subtle but because it taps into a universal fear: that love alone is not enough to protect us from loss. It reminds us that grief does not wait for old age or preparation and that even the most passionate connections must eventually contend with impermanence. In its simplicity, the film quietly teaches that loving deeply also means risking profound sorrow and that this risk is not a failure but the cost of connection itself.

A Man Called Otto *(2022, PG-13, 2 h 6 min)*

Starring: Tom Hanks, Mariana Treviño

Directed by: Marc Forster

Film Description

A Man Called Otto centers on Otto Anderson, a rigid, rule-bound widower, whose life collapses after the death of his beloved wife Sonya and his forced retirement. With his routines stripped away and his sense of purpose gone, Otto sinks into despair and repeatedly attempts suicide, convinced that life has nothing left to offer him.

Each attempt is interrupted by the arrival of new neighbors, particularly Marisol and her young family, whose chaotic warmth gradually cracks Otto's armor. Through reluctant relationships, acts of service, and unexpected connection, Otto begins to reengage with life. The film balances dark humor with tenderness, showing how grief can isolate people while also leaving openings for transformation when connection reenters the picture.

While the story includes multiple suicide attempts, its heart lies in illustrating how unresolved grief and loneliness can distort one's relationship with living and how meaning can return through community, responsibility, and love that extends beyond loss.

Mortality Themes

- Widower grief and loss of identity after a partner's death

- Suicide ideation and interrupted attempts

- The tension between wanting to die and wanting pain to stop

- Grief as both paralysis and potential transformation

- Rediscovering purpose through connection and service

Discussion Prompts

1. How does Otto's grief express itself differently than more outwardly emotional portrayals of mourning?

2. What role does routine play in Otto's identity and sense of control after loss?

3. How does community function as a protective factor against despair in the film?

4. What is the difference between Otto wanting to die and wanting relief from suffering?

5. How does the film handle humor alongside very serious themes of suicide and grief?

6. What moments in the film suggest that responsibility to others can reawaken a sense of purpose after grief?

Movie Pairings and Activities

- Pair the movie with *Gran Torino* (2008) or *Up* (2009) to compare gruff protagonists softened by unexpected relationships.

- Or pair it with *About Schmidt* (2002) to explore grief, aging, and purpose after retirement.

- Invite viewers to discuss how grief can shrink a life and what helps expand it again.

- Use the film to talk about warning signs of suicidal ideation in older adults.

Final Thought

A Man Called Otto reminds us that grief does not always look like tears or eloquent sorrow; sometimes it looks like bitterness, rigidity, and withdrawal from the world. The film gently suggests that, while we cannot fix grief, we can interrupt isolation. Otto's journey shows that meaning does not disappear with loss, but it often requires others to help us find it again. In choosing connection over resignation, Otto models how life can offer purpose even after profound heartbreak.

Manchester by the Sea *(2016, R, 2 h 17 min)*

Starring: Casey Affleck, Michelle Williams, Lucas Hedges

Directed by: Kenneth Lonergan

Film Description

Manchester by the Sea follows Lee Chandler, a withdrawn and emotionally shut-down handyman living a solitary life in Boston. When his older brother Joe dies suddenly of a heart condition, Lee is forced to return to his hometown of Manchester by the Sea to handle funeral arrangements and care for his teenage nephew Patrick. The return also brings him face-to-face with the devastating past he has worked relentlessly to avoid.

Years earlier, Lee survived an accidental house fire caused by his own negligence, a tragedy that killed his three young children and destroyed his marriage. The film unfolds these layers of loss gradually, mirroring how unresolved grief often resurfaces in fragments rather than tidy narratives. Lee functions day to day, but his grief is ever present, shaping his relationships, choices, and capacity for connection.

Rather than offering catharsis or redemption, the film presents grief as something that can be lived with but not necessarily overcome. It is an unflinching portrait of a man who continues breathing, working, and caring for others while carrying a sorrow that does not resolve.

Mortality Themes

- Compounded and layered losses
- Accidental death and survivor guilt
- Functional grief and emotional numbing
- Secondary losses including marriage, community, and identity
- The limits of healing and the reality of enduring grief

Discussion Prompts

1. How does Lee's grief differ from more cinematic portrayals of mourning and recovery?
2. What does the film suggest about the idea that grief must lead to growth or transformation?
3. How do guilt and responsibility complicate Lee's ability to heal?
4. In what ways does the town of Manchester serve as both a place of memory and a trigger for grief?
5. Is caring for Patrick an act of healing for Lee or simply an act of duty?
6. What does the film suggest about the difference between forgiveness and acceptance in the context of devastating loss?

Movie Pairings and Activities

- Pair the movie with *Ordinary People* (1980) to explore grief within families after accidental death.
- Or pair it with *Rabbit Hole* (2010) to examine parental loss and survivor guilt.
- Invite viewers to discuss the difference between surviving grief and resolving it.
- Use the film to open conversation about grief that does not follow a linear or hopeful arc.

Final Thought

Manchester by the Sea challenges the comforting notion that time heals all wounds. It offers a quieter truth: Some losses permanently alter who we are, and learning to live alongside that pain may be the most realistic form of resilience. The film honors those whose grief does not resolve neatly, reminding us that continuing to live, love imperfectly, and show up when we can is itself a profound act of courage.

Ordinary People *(1980, R, 2 h 4 min)*

Starring: Donald Sutherland, Mary Tyler Moore, Timothy Hutton, Judd Hirsch

Directed by: Robert Redford

Film Description

Ordinary People peels back the façade of a seemingly perfect upper-middle-class suburban family to reveal the quiet devastation left by loss. The Jarretts are reeling after the accidental death of their eldest son, Buck, in a boating accident. His younger brother Conrad survives the incident but is consumed by survivor guilt and spirals into depression, eventually attempting suicide.

As the family tries to return to normal life, their grief pulls them in opposite directions. Conrad begins therapy and slowly learns to articulate his pain, anger, and shame. His father Calvin struggles to hold the family together while questioning his own emotional distance. His mother Beth, fiercely committed to appearances and control, refuses to confront her grief at all, clinging to routine as a defense against emotional collapse.

The film is less about death itself and more about what happens when grief is expressed, denied, or mismanaged within a family system. With quiet intensity, *Ordinary People* shows how unresolved mourning can fracture relationships, how silence can be as damaging as loss, and how healing often begins when someone is finally willing to speak the truth.

Mortality Themes

- Sudden accidental death
- Survivor guilt and self-blame
- Family systems under stress
- Divergent grieving styles
- Therapy as a path toward healing
- Unresolved and disenfranchised grief

Discussion Prompts

1. How does each family member grieve differently, and how do those differences create conflict?

2. In what ways does Beth's refusal to engage with grief affect Conrad and Calvin?

3. How does therapy function as a lifeline for Conrad, and why is it threatening to the family dynamic?

4. What does the film suggest about the danger of prioritizing appearances over emotional honesty?

5. Is reconciliation possible without shared mourning, or does grief require mutual acknowledgment?

6. How does the film portray the cost of emotional avoidance compared to the risk of emotional honesty?

Movie Pairings and Activities

- Pair the movie with *Manchester by the Sea* (2016) to explore survivor guilt after accidental death.
- Or pair it with *Rabbit Hole* (2010) to compare parental grief and coping strategies.
- Invite viewers to reflect on how their own families handle emotional pain and silence.
- Use the film to spark conversation about therapy, especially for adolescents coping with loss.

Final Thought

Ordinary People reminds us that grief does not only live in tears and funerals, it lives in what is unsaid, in rigid routines, and in the pressure to appear "fine." The film gently but firmly argues that healing requires honesty, vulnerability, and the courage to face pain together. When grief is denied, families fracture. When it is acknowledged, even imperfectly, connection becomes possible again.

P.S. I Love You *(2007, PG-13, 2 h 6 min)*

Starring: Hilary Swank, Gerard Butler, Lisa Kudrow, Gina Gershon

Directed by: Richard LaGravenese

Film Description

P.S. I Love You follows Holly Kennedy, a young woman whose life is abruptly shattered by the death of her husband Gerry from a sudden illness. Overwhelmed by grief and struggling to imagine a future without him, Holly discovers that Gerry prepared a series of ten letters before his death. Each letter arrives at carefully timed intervals, offering encouragement, gentle nudges back into the world, and permission to keep living.

As Holly follows Gerry's posthumous guidance, she navigates awkward social expectations, well-meaning but sometimes clueless friends and family, and her own conflicted emotions about moving forward. The letters take her on emotional and literal journeys that help her reconnect with joy, friendship, creativity, and self-trust.

While undeniably romantic and occasionally wish fulfilling, the film resonates because it captures a common longing among mourners: the desire for reassurance, direction, and continued connection after loss. Beneath the fantasy is a relatable story about learning to carry love forward rather than leaving it behind.

Mortality Themes

- Sudden spousal loss
- Continuing bonds with the deceased

- The tension between holding on and letting go
- Social misunderstandings around grief
- Permission to experience joy after loss
- Grief as a process of identity reconstruction

Discussion Prompts

1. How do Gerry's letters help Holly move forward without erasing her grief?

2. In what ways do Holly's friends and family support her, and where do they fall short?

3. Does the idea of posthumous guidance feel comforting, unrealistic, or both?

4. How does the film portray the difference between "moving on" and "moving forward"?

5. What might healthy continuing bonds look like without relying on fantasy elements?

6. How might the story change if Holly had to find her way forward without Gerry's letters?

Movie Pairings and Activities

- Pair the film with *Truly, Madly, Deeply* (1990) to compare romantic afterlife fantasies.

- Or pair it with *A Man Called Otto* (2022) to explore different paths through spousal grief.

- Invite viewers to write a letter they wish they had received or one they would leave behind.

- Discuss cultural expectations about how long grief should last and how it should look.

Final Thought

P.S. I Love You reminds us that grief does not require us to sever our bonds with the dead to live well. Instead, it suggests that love can remain a companion rather than a chain. While few of us receive letters from beyond the grave, many carry internal messages from those we have loved. The challenge, as Holly learns, is allowing those messages to support a life that continues to unfold.

The Queen *(2006, PG-13, 1 h 43 min)*

Starring: Helen Mirren, Michael Sheen, James Cromwell

Directed by: Stephen Frears

Film Description

The Queen dramatizes the tense days following the sudden death of Princess Diana in 1997 when public grief in Britain reaches a historic and emotional intensity. As mourners flood the streets with flowers, handwritten notes, and tears, Queen Elizabeth II retreats to Balmoral Castle, adhering strictly to royal protocol and tradition. From her perspective, Diana is no longer a member of the royal family, and therefore her funeral should remain a private matter for the Spencer family.

Meanwhile, newly elected Prime Minister Tony Blair recognizes the magnitude of public sorrow and urges the Queen to respond in ways that acknowledge the nation's grief. The film unfolds as a quiet but powerful study of leadership under pressure, cultural expectations around mourning, and the collision between institutional restraint and emotional expression.

Rather than focusing on Diana herself, the story centers on how societies grieve collectively and how public figures navigate loss that is both personal and symbolic. Helen Mirren's Oscar-winning performance captures a monarch grappling with change, vulnerability, and the realization that rituals must sometimes evolve to meet the emotional needs of the living.

Mortality Themes

- Public versus private grief
- Collective mourning after a sudden death
- The role of ritual and symbolism in loss
- Tradition versus emotional expression

- Leadership during times of national grief

- Changing cultural expectations around death

Discussion Prompts

1. Why does the Queen initially resist public displays of mourning?

2. How does public grief differ from private grief, and why does it matter?

3. What role do rituals play in helping large groups process loss?

4. How does the film portray generational and cultural shifts in mourning practices?

5. What responsibilities do leaders have when a nation is grieving?

6. How does the film suggest that acknowledging grief can strengthen rather than undermine authority or leadership?

Movie Pairings and Activities

- Pair the film with *Ordinary People* (1980) to contrast public grief with private family mourning.

- Or pair it with *Manchester by the Sea* (2016) to explore different responses to loss.

- Discuss how social media has changed public mourning since 1997.

- Invite viewers to share memories of a public death that affected them personally.

Final Thought

The Queen reminds us that grief is not only an individual experience but also a communal one. When loss touches a nation, rituals become language, symbols become comfort, and acknowledgment becomes essential. The film gently argues that honoring grief is not a sign of weakness but an act of connection. In recognizing the pain of others, we affirm our shared humanity.

A Single Man *(2009, R, 1 h 39 min)*

Starring: Colin Firth, Julianne Moore, Nicholas Hoult

Directed by: Tom Ford

Film Description

Set in Los Angeles in 1962, *A Single Man* follows George Falconer, a British college professor, whose life has been hollowed out by the sudden death of his longtime partner, Jim, in a car accident eight months earlier. Because their relationship was never legally recognized and existed in a deeply homophobic era, George is excluded from Jim's funeral and denied the social permission to grieve openly.

The film unfolds over the course of a single day as George moves through his meticulously ordered life while privately contemplating whether he wants to continue living at all. His interactions with students, strangers, and his close friend Charley reveal the quiet, isolating weight of unacknowledged grief. Visual style and precise pacing mirror George's emotional restraint, while small moments of beauty and connection puncture his despair.

Rather than offering a traditional arc of healing, *A Single Man* presents grief as something lived internally and moment by moment. It honors the reality that mourning does not always have witnesses, rituals, or resolution, especially for those whose losses are marginalized by society.

Mortality Themes

- Disenfranchised grief
- Loss without ritual or social acknowledgment
- Isolation in mourning
- Suicidal ideation linked to unresolved grief
- Identity loss after the death of a partner
- The quiet persistence of love after death

Discussion Prompts

1. How does being denied mourning rituals affect George's grief process?

2. What is disenfranchised grief, and where do we see it today?

3. How does the film use stillness and routine to portray depression and loss?

4. In what ways do brief connections offer George moments of relief or meaning?

5. How might George's experience differ if the story were set in a different era?

6. How does the lack of social acknowledgement shape the intensity and direction of George's grief?

Movie Pairings and Activities

- Pair the movie with *The Hours* (2002) to explore internalized grief and existential despair.

- Or pair it with *Good Grief* (2023) to contrast public versus private mourning in LGBTQ+ stories.

- Invite discussion on how rituals validate grief and why they matter.

- Encourage viewers to reflect on losses that were not publicly recognized.

Final Thought

A Single Man gives voice to grief that exists in silence. It reminds us that not all losses are met with casseroles, sympathy cards, or ceremonies, yet they still reshape lives just as profoundly. The film challenges us to recognize whose grief is seen, whose is overlooked, and how much healing depends on being allowed to mourn openly. In honoring quiet sorrow, it asks us to widen our compassion and our understanding of what grief can look like.

Smoke Signals *(1998, PG-13, 1 h 29 min)*

Starring: Adam Beach, Evan Adams, Irene Bedard, Gary Farmer

Directed by: Chris Eyre

Written by: Sherman Alexie

Film Description

Smoke Signals is the first feature film written, directed, and produced by Native Americans, and it tells a deeply human story through humor, restraint, and cultural specificity. Starting on the Coeur d'Alene reservation, the film follows two young men, Victor Joseph and Thomas Builds-the-Fire, as they take a road trip from Idaho to Arizona and back to retrieve the cremated remains of Victor's estranged father, Arnold.

Victor carries anger, abandonment, and unresolved grief after years of emotional distance from his alcoholic father. Thomas, a gentle storyteller and social outsider, carries a different inheritance. He was saved as a baby by Arnold during a fire and feels gratitude rather than resentment. Their journey becomes less about transporting ashes and more about confronting competing narratives of loss, memory, and identity.

Along the way, the film explores how grief is shaped by culture, history, and intergenerational trauma. Storytelling functions as both burden and medicine, allowing truths to surface that had been buried beneath silence and pain. *Smoke Signals* offers a rare cinematic portrayal of indigenous grief that is neither romanticized nor flattened but lived, complex, and deeply communal.

Mortality Themes

- Parental loss and emotional abandonment
- Complicated and unresolved grief
- Intergenerational trauma
- Cremation and the return of remains
- Cultural identity and collective memory
- Storytelling as a tool for healing

Discussion Prompts

1. How do Victor and Thomas grieve the same man in very different ways?

2. What role does storytelling play in healing, and when can it feel like a burden?

3. How does intergenerational trauma shape Victor's anger and silence?

4. In what ways does community influence how grief is expressed or contained?

5. How does the road trip structure mirror the emotional journey of mourning?

6. What does the film suggest about the difference between truth and forgiveness in the grieving process?

Movie Pairings and Activities

- Pair the movie with *Manchester by the Sea* (2016) to explore unresolved parental grief and silence.

- Or pair it with *Bonneville* (2006), *Around the Bend* (2004) or *Elizabethtown* (2005) to compare road trips centered on cremated remains.

- Invite viewers to reflect on the stories they tell about their own losses.

- Discuss how cultural context shapes mourning rituals and expectations.

Final Thought

Smoke Signals reminds us that grief is rarely just about one death. It carries history, memory, and unanswered questions across generations. By honoring humor, storytelling, and cultural truth, the film shows that healing does not come from forgetting the past but from finally telling it out loud. In doing so, it offers a powerful model of how communities carry their dead and help the living move forward.

Steel Magnolias *(1989, PG, 1 h 57 min)*

Starring: Sally Field, Dolly Parton, Shirley MacLaine, Olympia Dukakis, Daryl Hannah, Julia Roberts

Directed by: Herbert Ross

Film Description

Set in a small Louisiana town, *Steel Magnolias* centers on a tight-knit group of women whose lives intersect in a beauty salon that functions as both a community hub and an emotional refuge. At the heart of the story is Shelby, a young woman with Type 1 diabetes, who chooses to pursue pregnancy despite serious medical risks. Her decision is made with love and hope, but it leads to devastating consequences.

The film moves fluidly between sharp humor and profound sorrow, showing how everyday moments of connection help sustain people through unimaginable loss. When Shelby dies following childbirth, her mother M'Lynn and the women around her must find ways to survive grief together. The salon becomes a place where tears and laughter coexist, where blunt honesty is allowed, and where no one grieves alone.

Rather than focusing solely on death itself, *Steel Magnolias* explores the long aftermath of loss, especially maternal grief. It portrays how community, ritual, and shared history help carry people forward when words fail. The film remains a touchstone for its honest depiction of how humor can be both a shield and a lifeline in the face of tragedy.

Mortality Themes

- Chronic illness and medical risk
- Maternal grief and the loss of an adult child
- Anticipatory grief
- Community support in mourning
- Humor as a coping mechanism
- Women bearing witness to one another's pain

Discussion Prompts

1. How does Shelby's choice to pursue pregnancy complicate the way we think about risk and autonomy?

2. In what ways does the salon function as a grieving space after Shelby's death?

3. How does humor help the characters survive loss without minimizing it?

4. How is maternal grief portrayed differently than other forms of mourning in the film?

5. What role does friendship play in making grief survivable?

6. How does shared history among the women change the way grief is expressed and received?

Movie Pairings and Activities

- Pair the film with *Terms of Endearment* (1983) to compare portrayals of maternal grief and illness.

- Or pair it with *Calendar Girls* (2003) to explore how female community responds to loss.

- Invite viewers to reflect on who shows up for them in times of grief and how.

- Discuss how shared spaces can become informal places of mourning and healing.

Final Thought

Steel Magnolias reminds us that grief does not arrive quietly or politely; it crashes into daily life, often alongside casseroles, jokes, and bad haircuts. By honoring both the sorrow and the laughter that follow a loss, the film offers a powerful truth: Strength is not the absence of tears but the courage to keep showing up for one another when hearts are breaking.

Truly Madly Deeply *(1990, PG, 1 h 46 min)*

Starring: Juliet Stevenson, Alan Rickman

Directed by: Anthony Minghella

Film Description

Nina is overwhelmed by grief after the sudden death of her partner Jamie. She withdraws from life, barely functioning in an apartment that has become a shrine to loss. Just when her loneliness feels unbearable, Jamie reappears, not alive but very much present as a ghost. At first, his return feels like a gift. Nina gets the comfort, affection, and familiarity she has been aching for, along with the chance to say everything left unsaid.

The fantasy quickly becomes complicated. Jamie is no longer evolving, while Nina slowly begins to heal. His presence keeps her tethered to the past, and his growing entourage of ghostly friends turns her home into a strange limbo where grief lingers instead of moving. What begins as wish fulfillment reveals the emotional cost of clinging to what was instead of allowing space for what might be.

The film gently explores how love does not disappear when someone dies but how living requires letting grief change shape. With humor, tenderness, and emotional honesty, *Truly Madly Deeply* shows that healing does not mean forgetting. It means learning how to carry love forward without being trapped by it.

Mortality Themes

- Acute grief after the death of a partner
- Unfinished emotional business
- The fantasy of continued connection after death
- Letting go versus holding on
- Identity rebuilding after loss
- Choosing life again after grief

Discussion Prompts

1. Why does Jamie's return feel comforting at first, and when does it begin to feel limiting?

2. How does the film distinguish between remembering someone and being stuck in grief?

3. What does Nina gain, and eventually lose, by having Jamie remain present?

4. How does humor soften the film's exploration of profound sorrow?

5. What does healthy letting go look like in the context of deep love?

6. At what point does comfort become an obstacle to healing in Nina's grief journey?

Movie Pairings and Activities

- Pair the film with *Ghost* (1990) to compare romantic afterlife fantasies and unresolved grief.

- Or pair it with *P.S. I Love You* (2007) to explore different visions of ongoing connection after death.

- Invite viewers to reflect on what they would want said or resolved if given one more conversation.

- Discuss how grief can keep us emotionally "haunted" even without ghosts.

Final Thought

Truly Madly Deeply captures a universal longing in grief: the wish for just one more moment. It reminds us that, while love may endure beyond death, living fully requires allowing grief to loosen its grip. Healing does not mean saying goodbye to love. It means giving love room to grow into something new.

Grief and Growth: Closing Thoughts

If this chapter teaches anything, it is that grief does not end. It evolves. Love does not disappear when someone dies, but it does change its shape. These films show that growth does not mean leaving grief behind. It means learning how to carry it differently, with more compassion for ourselves and others.

Grief can isolate, but it can also deepen connection. It can shatter assumptions and create unexpected openings for meaning, courage, and tenderness. Whether through friendship, creativity, community, or quiet acceptance, the characters in these stories discover that life after loss is still life, still worth living, and still capable of joy.

If these films prompt tears, reflection, or a recognition of your own story within them, they have done their work. Grief asks us to slow down, to remember, and to honor what mattered. Growth comes not from forgetting but from allowing love to continue even in the presence of loss.

MORTALITY AND LIVING FULLY

Introduction

These films begin with an uncomfortable truth: Awareness of death changes how we live. Whether prompted by illness, aging, grief, or a sudden confrontation with loss, the characters in this chapter find themselves standing at the edge of mortality and asking the same essential question: *What do I do with the time I have left?*

Some respond with bucket lists and bold choices. Others move more quietly, reexamining relationships, regrets, and the stories they tell about their lives. Not every character becomes braver or wiser overnight, and not every ending is neat. What unites these films is their insistence that mortality is not merely an ending but a clarifying force. When death enters the room, priorities shift. Truth emerges. Meaning demands attention.

These movies invite viewers to consider how acknowledging impermanence can deepen joy, foster connection, and inspire intention. They challenge the idea that thinking about death is morbid. Instead, they suggest it may be one of the most life-affirming acts we can engage in.

About Schmidt *(2002, R, 2 h 5 min)*

Starring: Jack Nicholson, Kathy Bates

Directed by: Alexander Payne

Film Description

After retiring from a long, predictable career in the insurance industry, Warren Schmidt finds his carefully ordered life unraveling when his wife of forty-two years dies suddenly. Left alone in a house full of silence and routine, Schmidt embarks on a cross-country RV trip to attend his estranged daughter's wedding. Along the way, he confronts his marriage, his parenting, his regrets, and the uncomfortable realization that much of his life has been lived on autopilot. Director Alexander Payne grounds the story in realism, including a memorable scene with real-life funeral director Tom Belford of John A. Gentleman Mortuaries in Omaha explaining the Federal Trade Commission's Funeral Rule to Schmidt.

Mortality Themes

- Identity loss after retirement and spousal death
- Late-life grief and loneliness
- Regret, legacy, and the search for meaning
- Awakening to life's emotional truths after loss

Discussion Prompts

1. How does Schmidt's grief show up differently than the more overt portrayals we often see on screen?

2. In what ways does retirement function as a kind of symbolic death in the film?

3. What does Schmidt's journey suggest about the possibility of growth later in life?

4. How does Schmidt's letter-writing function as both a search for meaning and a way to feel seen?

5. What moments suggest that it's never too late to change, even if the changes are small or imperfect?

- How does the film challenge cultural ideas about productivity equaling worth?

Movie Pairings and Activities

- Pair the movie with *Nebraska* (2013) to explore aging, regret, and family reconciliation.

- Invite viewers to write a short letter to their younger or future self about what they hope will matter the most.

Final Thought

About Schmidt reminds us that mortality is not only about dying; it is also about the quiet reckonings that arrive when roles fall away and we are left to ask whether we truly lived. Sometimes it takes loss to wake us up, and sometimes that awakening arrives later than we expected, but it arrives all the same.

Amélie *(2001, R, 2 h 2 min)*

Starring: Audrey Tautou, Mathieu Kassovitz

Directed by: Jean-Pierre Jeunet

Film Description

Set in the Montmartre neighborhood of Paris, *Amélie* follows a shy, imaginative young woman who quietly dedicates herself to improving the lives of others through small anonymous acts of kindness. While she orchestrates joy for strangers, coworkers, and neighbors, Amélie keeps herself at a careful emotional distance from intimacy and risk. Two deaths shake her out of her isolation: the sudden death of Princess Diana, which coincides with a pivotal childhood moment, and the earlier loss of her mother, which shaped her guarded worldview. These moments of mortality become catalysts, pushing Amélie to confront her fear of connection and step fully into life and love.

Mortality Themes

- Awareness of life's fragility
- Regret and the cost of emotional isolation

- Missed opportunities and the passage of time

- Choosing engagement over observation

Discussion Prompts

1. How does Amélie's relationship with death influence her decision to help others rather than herself?

2. In what ways does the film suggest that living fully requires emotional risk?

3. How do small moments and choices accumulate into a meaningful life?

4. What fears keep Amélie observing life instead of participating in it?

5. How does the film suggest that joy can be cultivated intentionally rather than discovered accidentally?

6. What might Amélie's story suggest about the difference between kindness as avoidance and kindness as connection?

Movie Pairings and Activities

- Pair the movie with *Stranger Than Fiction* (2006) to explore awakening to life through narrative awareness.

- Invite viewers to identify one small act of kindness or courage they have postponed and reflect on why.

Final Thought

Amélie gently reminds us that mortality is not only about endings; it is also about the quiet urgency to step out from the sidelines of our own lives. Time passes whether we engage with it or not, and joy often waits just beyond the risks we are afraid to take.

Around the Bend *(2004, R, 1 h 25 min)*

Starring: Christopher Walken, Michael Caine, Josh Lucas

Directed by: Jordan Roberts

Film Description

Around the Bend follows four generations of men brought together by the death of their patriarch, Henry Lair. Rather than a traditional funeral, Henry leaves behind a set of unconventional final wishes involving his cremated remains and a cross-country road trip. As the men travel together, long-standing estrangements, unspoken resentments, and buried grief surface. What begins as a logistical task becomes a reckoning with legacy, masculinity, and how families pass down both love and emotional silence. The road trip provides space for reflection, reconciliation, and the possibility of healing before time runs out.

Mortality Themes

- Planning unconventional funeral and disposition wishes
- Legacy beyond material inheritance
- Male grief and emotional restraint
- Reconciliation across generations
- Mortality as an invitation to repair relationships

Discussion Prompts

1. How does Henry's planned farewell differ from traditional funerals, and what does it offer his family emotionally?

2. In what ways does the film portray generational differences in how men express or suppress grief?

3. What unfinished business might still be resolved if families talked more openly about death and legacy?

4. How does physical movement (the road trip) help create emotional movement for the characters?

5. What does the film suggest about the cost of emotional silence passed down through generations?

6. How might Henry's approach to death change how his family remembers him, for better or worse?

Movie Pairings and Activities

- Pair the movie with *Bonneville* (2006) or *Elizabethtown* (2005) to compare ash-scattering road trips as catalysts for transformation.

- Encourage viewers to write down one value, story, or intention they would want future generations to understand about them.

Final Thought

Around the Bend suggests that death does not only close a chapter; when approached with intention, it can also reopen conversations that were long avoided. By naming our wishes and our feelings while we are still here, we give the people we love something far more lasting than instructions. We give them clarity, connection, and the chance to heal.

The Best Exotic Marigold Hotel *(2011, PG-13, 2 h 4 min)*

Starring: Judi Dench, Maggie Smith, Bill Nighy, Tom Wilkinson, Celia Imrie, Dev Patel

Directed by: John Madden

Film Description

A group of British retirees, each facing a crossroads brought on by aging, loss, or financial strain, relocate to India after being enticed by advertisements for a luxury retirement hotel. The hotel is far from what was promised, but the unfamiliar environment forces each character to confront fears about growing older, irrelevance, and unfinished life chapters. As relationships form and expectations shift, the residents discover that later life can still offer love, purpose, and transformation. What begins as an escape from decline becomes an invitation to engage more fully with life.

Mortality Themes

- Aging and fear of decline
- Reinvention and late-life identity
- Grief and starting over after loss
- Legacy beyond productivity
- Acceptance of impermanence and change

Discussion Prompts

1. How does each character's relationship with aging influence their choices and outlook on life?

2. What assumptions about "retirement" or later life does the film challenge?

3. How does embracing uncertainty open the door to meaning rather than fear?

4. How does dislocation from familiar environments help the characters reimagine who they can become?

5. What fears about aging are reinforced and which are dismantled by the film?

6. How does the movie redefine success later in life beyond financial security or status?

Movie Pairings and Activities

- Pair the movie with *About Schmidt* (2002) to explore retirement as both loss and opportunity.
- Invite viewers to reflect on what a meaningful "next chapter" might look like for them, regardless of age.

Final Thought

The Best Exotic Marigold Hotel gently reminds us that, while aging narrows some possibilities, it widens others. Mortality is not only about endings; it is also about choosing curiosity over fear and engagement over withdrawal. As one character wisely observes, everything will be all right in the end. And if it is not all right, it is not yet the end.

The Big Chill *(1983, R, 1 h 45 min)*

Starring: Glenn Close, William Hurt, Jeff Goldblum, Tom Berenger, Mary Kay Place, Meg Tilly, Kevin Kline, JoBeth Williams

Directed by: Lawrence Kasdan

Film Description

A close-knit group of college friends reunites for a weekend after the suicide of their friend Alex. Now in their thirties, they gather at a South Carolina home to mourn his death, attend the funeral, and reconnect after years of drifting apart. As the weekend unfolds, conversations, conflicts, laughter, and music reveal not only their grief for Alex but also a deeper mourning for the ideals, ambitions, and identities they once held. The funeral becomes a catalyst for self-examination as each character confronts where life has taken them and what may still be possible.

Mortality Themes

- Suicide and collective grief
- Loss of youthful identity and unmet expectations
- Existential reckoning at midlife
- Regret and the "road not taken"
- Humor and nostalgia as coping mechanisms

Discussion Prompts

1. In what ways are the characters grieving Alex, and in what ways are they grieving versions of themselves?

2. How does the film portray the tension between youthful ideals and adult compromises?

3. What role does humor play in helping the group navigate grief and discomfort?

4. How does the group's shared past both support and trap them emotionally?

5. What does the film suggest about the role of friendship in navigating midlife reckoning?

6. If Alex's death is a wake-up call, what different "alarms" do the characters hear or ignore?

Movie Pairings and Activities

- Pair the film with *Ordinary People* (1980) to explore different portrayals of suicide and family or communal responses to loss.

- Invite viewers to reflect on which parts of their younger selves they miss and which they are glad to have outgrown.

Final Thought

The Big Chill reminds us that death does not only arrive in the form of a funeral; it also shows up quietly in abandoned dreams, altered friendships, and the realization that time has passed whether we noticed it or not. Yet within that reckoning lies an invitation: to reconnect, to forgive ourselves and others, and to decide how we want to live with the time still ahead.

Big Fish *(2003, PG-13, 2 h 5 min)*

Starring: Ewan McGregor, Albert Finney, Billy Crudup, Jessica Lange, Helena Bonham Carter

Directed by: Tim Burton

Film Description

As his father Edward Bloom lies dying, journalist Will Bloom struggles to reconcile the man he knows with the larger-than-life storyteller his father has always been. Edward's life is told through fantastical tales filled with giants, witches, circuses, and impossible adventures; stories Will dismisses as exaggerations and evasions. As the end approaches, father and son inch toward understanding, discovering that emotional truth may matter more than factual accuracy. The film unfolds like a cinematic Irish wake, rich with humor, myth, and affection, suggesting that the stories we tell shape how we are remembered.

Mortality Themes

- Legacy through storytelling
- Anticipatory grief and dying well
- Parent-child reconciliation
- Memory, myth, and emotional truth
- Immortality through meaning rather than facts

Discussion Prompts

1. Why is Will so invested in separating truth from fiction in his father's stories?
2. How do stories function as a form of legacy in this film?
3. What does the ending suggest about how we might want to be remembered?
4. How does the film distinguish between emotional truth and factual truth, and why does that matter near the end of life?
5. What role does forgiveness play in the reconciliation between Will and Edward?
6. How might embracing myth over precision change how we tell our own life stories?

Movie Pairings and Activities

- Pair the film with *About Schmidt* (2002) or *The Man Who Shot Liberty Valance* (1962) to compare different approaches to legacy and late-life reflection.
- Invite viewers to share a favorite family story and discuss what emotional truth it carries, even if the details may be embellished.

Final Thought

Big Fish gently reminds us that a life is not only measured by facts, dates, and accomplishments but by the meaning we leave behind. In the end, Edward Bloom does not ask to be remembered accurately, only lovingly. The film suggests that, when death approaches, reconciliation and story may matter more than certainty and that being remembered as larger than life can be its own quiet form of immortality.

Boys on the Side *(1995, R, 1 h 55 min)*

Starring: Whoopi Goldberg, Mary-Louise Parker, Drew Barrymore

Directed by: Herbert Ross

Film Description

Three women who begin as near strangers form an unexpected bond during a cross-country road trip. Jane is living with HIV and facing a terminal prognosis, Robin is searching for stability after leaving an abusive relationship, and Holly is escaping legal trouble and emotional chaos. As their journey unfolds, the road trip becomes a temporary sanctuary where friendship, honesty, and care emerge naturally. The film balances humor with heartbreak, showing how chosen family can form quickly when mortality is present and time feels precious.

Mortality Themes

- Living with terminal illness
- Anticipatory grief
- Found family and chosen support systems
- Caregiving and companionship at end of life
- Humor and humanity in the face of dying

Discussion Prompts

1. How does the presence of Jane's illness shape the relationships among the women?

2. What does the film suggest about the role of friendship when traditional family structures are absent or insufficient?

3. How does humor function as both connection and coping throughout the story?

4. How does time-limited living intensify honesty and intimacy in the group?

5. What does the film suggest about caregiving as a reciprocal experience rather than a one-way sacrifice?

6. How might the story change if the women had never taken the road trip at all?

Movie Pairings and Activities

- Pair the movie with *Steel Magnolias* (1989) to explore how female friendships hold space for grief and resilience.

- Invite participants to reflect on who has functioned as "chosen family" during difficult times in their own lives.

Final Thought

Boys on the Side reminds us that dying does not happen in isolation. Even when a life is shortened, meaning can expand through connection, laughter, and care. The film offers a compassionate vision of end-of-life support rooted not in perfection or preparedness but in showing up for one another, mile after mile.

The Bucket List *(2007, PG-13, 1 h 37 min)*

Starring: Jack Nicholson, Morgan Freeman

Directed by: Rob Reiner

Film Description

Two men from very different walks of life meet in a hospital room after receiving terminal cancer diagnoses. Carter Chambers is a quiet, intelligent mechanic who has spent his life putting responsibilities first. Edward Cole is a wealthy sharp-tongued businessman used to getting his way. When they realize their remaining time is limited, they create a "bucket list" of experiences they want to have before they die. Their global road trip becomes less about skydiving and safaris and more about friendship, forgiveness, love, and reckoning with unfinished emotional business.

Mortality Themes

- Awareness of limited time

- Living fully in the face of terminal illness

- Friendship and connection near the end of life

- Legacy, meaning, and reflection

- Preferences for death care and cremation

Discussion Prompts

1. How does knowing they are dying change the way the men relate to each other and to the world?

2. What moments on the bucket list turn out to matter more than the adventures themselves?

3. How does the film balance lighthearted humor with serious reflections on death?

4. How do Carter and Edward redefine "success" as their friendship deepens?

5. What does the film suggest about reconciliation as part of living fully, not just dying well?

6. How might the idea of a bucket list limit living, even as it inspires it?

Movie Pairings and Activities

- Pair the movie with *About Schmidt* (2002) to explore late-life reflection and reassessment after loss or diagnosis.

- Invite participants to create a personal "life values list" rather than a bucket list, focusing on relationships, experiences, or conversations they want to prioritize now.

Final Thought

The Bucket List offers a gentle reminder that mortality has a way of clarifying what truly matters. While not everyone will chase big adventures, the film suggests that the real work of dying well often involves connection, honesty, and the courage to say what has been left unsaid. Sometimes the most meaningful journeys happen long before the final destination.

Hannah and Her Sisters *(1986, PG-13, 1 h 47 min)*

Starring: Woody Allen, Mia Farrow, Michael Caine, Dianne Wiest, Barbara Hershey

Directed by: Woody Allen

Film Description

Set over the course of two years and framed by Thanksgiving gatherings, this ensemble comedy drama follows the interconnected lives of three sisters and the people who love them. At the center is Hannah, the emotional anchor of the family. Running alongside the romantic entanglements and shifting relationships is Mickey, Hannah's former husband, a neurotic television producer who experiences a health scare that sends him spiraling into an existential crisis. Confronted with the possibility of death, Mickey searches for meaning through medicine, philosophy, and religion before stumbling upon a more unexpected answer.

Mortality Themes

- Fear of death and health anxiety
- Existential crisis and the search for meaning
- Mortality as a catalyst for spiritual questioning
- Joy, art, and connection as responses to despair
- Acceptance of life's uncertainty

Discussion Prompts

1. How does Mickey's health scare change his outlook on life and meaning?

2. What does the film suggest about where people actually find purpose when traditional belief systems fall short?

3. How do relationships, family, and everyday joys function as antidotes to existential fear?

4. Why does Mickey's search for meaning fail when it is driven by fear rather than curiosity?

5. How does the film suggest that meaning can emerge accidentally rather than through intention?

6. What role does gratitude play in easing existential anxiety by the end of the story?

Movie Pairings and Activities

- Pair the movie with *Stranger Than Fiction* (2006) to compare how awareness of mortality prompts life changes.

- Invite viewers to reflect on what brings them comfort or meaning when confronted with uncertainty about health or death.

Final Thought

Hannah and Her Sisters suggests that, while mortality can provoke terror and obsessive searching, it can also sharpen our appreciation for life's small pleasures. Rather than offering grand spiritual answers, the film gently proposes that laughter, love, art, and connection may be enough. Sometimes meaning is not discovered through belief but through participation in life itself.

Last Holiday *(2006, PG-13, 1 h 52 min)*

Starring: Queen Latifah, Gérard Depardieu, LL Cool J, Timothy Hutton

Directed by: Wayne Wang

Film Description

Georgia Byrd is a quiet, cautious department store employee who lives a careful, restrained life, saving her dreams in a scrapbook rather than acting on them. When she is mistakenly diagnosed with a terminal illness and told she has only weeks to live, Georgia decides she has nothing to lose. She cashes in her savings and travels to a luxurious European resort where she embraces pleasure, honesty, and generosity for the first time. Free from the fear of the future, she becomes her most authentic self, deeply affecting everyone she meets along the way.

Mortality Themes

- Death awareness as a catalyst for transformation
- Living fully versus living safely
- The power of kindness and generosity
- Regret, postponed dreams, and second chances
- Authenticity in the face of limited time

Discussion Prompts

1. How does Georgia's belief that she is dying change the way she treats herself and others?

2. What fears keep Georgia living small before her diagnosis, and which of those fears feel familiar?

3. If you believed your time were limited, what choices might you make differently?

4. How does Georgia's honesty disrupt social hierarchies and expectations around politeness?

5. What does the film suggest about generosity as a form of fully living?

6. How might Georgia's transformation have unfolded differently if she had not believed death was imminent?

Movie Pairings and Activities

- Pair the movie with *The Bucket List* (2007) to compare different approaches to living fully near the end of life.
- Invite viewers to create their own "living now" list, not a bucket list for someday but small changes they could make this year.

Final Thought

Last Holiday reminds us that it should not take a terminal diagnosis, real or imagined, to give ourselves the permission to live with courage and joy. The film gently nudges us to ask an uncomfortable but liberating question: If we waited until we were dying to start living, what have we been waiting for all along?

The Last Word *(2017, R, 1 h 48 min)*

Starring: Shirley MacLaine, Amanda Seyfried, AnnJewel Lee Dixon, Thomas Sadoski

Directed by: Mark Pellington

Film Description

Harriet Lauler is a wealthy recently retired businesswoman who has spent her life in control, efficiency, and emotional distance. Concerned about how she will be remembered, Harriet hires a young journalist to write her obituary while she is still very much alive. When she reads the brutally honest first draft and realizes she is widely disliked and deeply disconnected, Harriet decides to take charge of her legacy while she still can. What follows is an awkward, funny, and unexpectedly tender attempt to repair relationships, form new ones, and reshape the story of her life before it is finalized.

Mortality Themes

- Legacy and how we are remembered
- Reinvention late in life
- Control versus connection
- Regret, reconciliation, and second chances
- Writing one's own ending while there is still time

Discussion Prompts

1. How does reading her own obituary force Harriet to confront the emotional cost of her choices?

2. What does the film suggest about the difference between professional success and a meaningful life?

3. If someone wrote your obituary today, what surprises might it contain?

4. What fears about vulnerability keep Harriet emotionally distant early in the film?

5. How does witnessing the lives of others begin to soften Harriet's sense of control?

6. What does the film suggest about legacy as an ongoing practice rather than a final verdict?

Movie Pairings and Activities

- Pair the movie with *About Schmidt* (2002) to explore how retirement and loss can spark late-life self-examination.

- Invite viewers to draft a "living obituary" focused on values they want reflected, not accomplishments alone.

Final Thought

The Last Word offers a gently comic but serious reminder that legacy is not something decided after death. It is shaped every day, through how we show up for others. The film reassures us that, while we cannot rewrite our past chapters, we often have more time than we think to revise the ending.

Mr. Magorium's Wonder Emporium *(2007, G, 1 h 33 min)*

Starring: Dustin Hoffman, Natalie Portman, Jason Bateman

Directed by: Zach Helm

Film Description

At first glance, this whimsical fantasy appears to be a children's movie about a magical toy store. At its heart, however, it is a gentle meditation on mortality and transition. Mr. Magorium is a 243-year-old eccentric genius who knows his life is nearing its natural end. Rather than resisting death, he prepares carefully, choosing his successor and trusting that life will continue without him. When he dies, the toy store itself seems to mourn, falling into chaos and decay. It is only when his young manager, Molly Mahoney, embraces her creativity and confidence that the store is restored. The story frames death not as an ending but as a necessary passage that allows renewal to occur.

Mortality Themes

- Peaceful acceptance of death
- Legacy and succession
- Grief expressed through disruption and change
- Renewal through creativity and courage
- Trusting life to continue without us

Discussion Prompts

1. How does Mr. Magorium's calm acceptance of death differ from how death is usually portrayed in films?

2. In what ways does the toy store reflect the emotional state of those left behind?

3. What does the film suggest about the responsibility of those who inherit a legacy?

4. What fears or doubts keep Molly from stepping fully into her role before Mr. Magorium's death?

5. How does the film distinguish between preserving a legacy and freezing it in time?

6. What does accepting succession require emotionally from both the one leaving and the one staying?

Movie Pairings and Activities

- Pair the movie with *Coco* (2017) to explore how remembrance and creativity sustain life beyond death.
- Invite participants to reflect on what they would want to pass on, skills, values, or responsibilities, rather than possessions.

Final Thought

Mr. Magorium's Wonder Emporium reminds us that death does not extinguish meaning. It creates space for others to step forward. By showing a death that is anticipated, accepted, and even celebrated, the film offers a comforting vision of mortality as a handoff rather than a loss.

On Golden Pond *(1981, PG, 1 h 49 min)*

Starring: Henry Fonda, Katharine Hepburn, Jane Fonda

Directed by: Mark Rydell

Film Description

Set during what may be their final summer at a beloved lake house in New England, *On Golden Pond* follows Norman and Ethel Thayer as they confront aging in very different ways. Norman, sharp-tongued and increasingly forgetful, struggles with memory loss and the quiet terror of physical and cognitive decline. Ethel remains warm, playful, and fiercely committed to finding joy in each passing day. When their estranged daughter Chelsea arrives with her teenage stepson, old wounds surface, and the lake becomes a backdrop for reconciliation, reflection, and reckoning. The film unfolds slowly, allowing space for humor, tenderness, frustration and the unspoken understanding that time is finite.

Mortality Themes

- Aging and cognitive decline
- Anticipatory grief and end-of-life awareness
- Intergenerational conflict and reconciliation
- The passage of time and changing identities
- Choosing connection over fear

Discussion Prompts

1. How do Norman and Ethel model different emotional responses to aging and mortality?

2. What role does memory, both preserved and fading, play in shaping identity in the film?

3. How does the lake setting function as a metaphor for life, continuity, and impermanence?

4. How does humor function as both defense and connection for Norman throughout the film?

5. What unfinished emotional business exists between Norman and Chelsea, and why does time pressure matter?

6. How does the film suggest we can live fully even as physical and cognitive abilities change?

Movie Pairings and Activities

- Pair the film with *About Schmidt* (2002) to explore late-life reflection and strained parent-child relationships.

- Invite viewers to reflect on a place that holds deep personal meaning and how it connects them to different stages of life.

Final Thought

On Golden Pond offers a quiet, honest portrait of growing old without sentimentality or despair. It reminds us that, even as bodies weaken and memories falter, the capacity for love, repair, and humor remains. Mortality here is not dramatic or heroic. It is gentle, persistent, and deeply human.

The Seventh Seal *(1958, Not Rated, 1 h 36 min)*

Starring: Max von Sydow, Bengt Ekerot, Bibi Andersson

Directed by: Ingmar Bergman

Film Description

Set in medieval Europe during the Black Plague, *The Seventh Seal* follows knight Antonius Block as he returns from the Crusades to a land ravaged by death, fear, and spiritual uncertainty. Upon his arrival, he encounters death itself, personified as a pale calm figure who challenges him to a game of chess. The game becomes a temporary reprieve, buying Block time to search for meaning, certainty, and evidence of God in a world that appears abandoned. Along the road, Block and his squire encounter flagellants, terrified villagers, and a troupe of traveling performers whose simple joy, love, and art offer a stark contrast to despair. The film unfolds as a meditation on faith, doubt, fear, and the inevitability of death.

Mortality Themes

- The inevitability of death
- Fear of death versus acceptance
- Crisis of faith and spiritual doubt
- The search for meaning in a fragile world
- Art, love, and human connection as responses to mortality

Discussion Prompts

1. Why does Antonius Block challenge Death to a game of chess rather than resist him outright?
2. How do the traveling performers offer a different philosophy of living and dying than the knight?
3. What does the film suggest about the role of faith, or the absence of it, in facing mortality?
4. How does Antonius Block's fear of meaninglessness differ from a fear of death itself?
5. Why are the moments with the performers often quieter, lighter, and more satisfying than the knight's spiritual struggles?
6. What does the film suggest counts as a "win" when death is inevitable?

Movie Pairings and Activities

- Pair the film with *Bill and Ted's Bogus Journey* (1991) to explore how the chess-with-death motif shifts from existential dread to comic absurdity.
- Invite viewers to reflect on what gives their life meaning when certainty is unavailable.

Final Thought

The Seventh Seal is not simply about dying; it is about living with the knowledge that death is unavoidable. Bergman offers no easy answers, only the invitation to sit with uncertainty and choose how we live in the face of it. Even as death claims everyone in the end, the film quietly suggests that moments of kindness, art, and love may be victories of their own.

The Way *(2010, PG-13, 2 h 3 min)*

Starring: Martin Sheen, Emilio Estevez, Deborah Kara Unger, James Nesbitt

Directed by: Emilio Estevez

Film Description

When his estranged adult son dies suddenly while hiking the Camino de Santiago in northern Spain, American ophthalmologist Tom Avery travels overseas to recover the body. Instead of bringing his son home, Tom makes an unexpected decision to carry his ashes and complete the pilgrimage his son began. What starts as a reluctant act of obligation becomes a slow embodied journey through grief. Along the way, Tom joins a small mismatched group of fellow pilgrims, each walking for their own reasons. As miles accumulate, grief softens into reflection, isolation gives way to connection, and physical movement mirrors inner change. The Camino becomes not just a destination but a container for mourning, memory, and quiet healing.

Mortality Themes

- Parental loss and unresolved relationships
- Ritual journeys as containers for grief
- Continuing bonds with the dead
- Grief as a physical and emotional process
- Transformation through community and shared experience

Discussion Prompts

1. Why does Tom decide to walk the Camino rather than return home immediately?

2. How does carrying his son's ashes change Tom's relationship to both grief and memory?

3. What role do fellow pilgrims play in Tom's healing even when words are few?

4. How does walking function differently from talking as a grief response for Tom?

5. What does the Camino offer that traditional mourning rituals may not?

6. How does the film portray transformation without forcing closure or resolution?

Movie Pairings and Activities

- Pair the movie with *Wild* (2014) to explore solo and communal journeys as responses to loss.

- Invite viewers to reflect on rituals, trips, or physical acts that have helped them process grief.

Final Thought

The Way reminds us that grief does not always move through conversation or tears alone. Sometimes it moves through footsteps, shared meals, and the quiet companionship of strangers. In choosing to walk rather than withdraw, Tom learns that healing does not erase loss but it can transform it into connection, meaning, and forward motion.

Mortality and Living Fully: Closing Thoughts

If mortality is the great equalizer, then living fully is the great response. The stories in this chapter show that confronting death does not shrink life; it expands it. Characters learn to love more honestly, forgive more freely, take risks they once postponed, and notice beauty they previously rushed past.

These films do not promise that life will be longer or easier once we face mortality. What they offer instead is depth, a reminder that time is precious because it is finite and that meaning is not found by avoiding death but by letting its presence sharpen how we choose to live.

If these stories leave you reflecting on your own unfinished conversations, deferred dreams, or quiet longings, they have done their work. Mortality, after all, is not just something that happens at the end of life; it is something that can guide us toward living more deliberately, compassionately, and fully, starting now.

ANIMATED FILMS

Introduction

Animated films have a unique ability to approach death sideways, with color, metaphor, music, and imagination softening the blow of some of life's hardest truths. For many people, these stories provide their very first encounter with loss, grief, and mortality. A parent dies. A friend disappears. A beloved figure is remembered through a ritual, song, or story. Because animation creates emotional distance from realism, it allows viewers of all ages to engage with profound ideas safely and honestly.

These films often speak in symbols rather than speeches: a house that will not move, a river of glowing ancestors, a child learning that sadness has a purpose. Animation gives form to feelings that are difficult to name, making it especially powerful in death education. What might feel overwhelming in live-action becomes approachable, even tender, when told through animated worlds.

Importantly, these films are not "just for kids." They frequently address adult concerns such as parental loss, survivor guilt, aging, legacy, and the challenge of continuing life after profound change. They invite intergenerational conversations, allowing children and adults to watch together and take away different, equally meaningful insights.

Bambi *(1942, G, 1 h 9 min)*

Starring: (voices) Hardie Albright, Stan Alexander, Sterling Holloway

Directed by: David Hand (supervising director)

Film Description

Disney gave generations of children their first cinematic encounter with death through the devastating loss of Bambi's mother. After she is killed by a hunter, young Bambi must navigate a world that suddenly feels unsafe and unfamiliar. Guided from a distance by his stoic father, the Great Prince of the Forest, Bambi grows from a vulnerable fawn into a mature stag who eventually takes on responsibility for the forest himself. The film uses nature as both the setting and the teacher, showing how life, death, danger, and renewal are inseparable parts of the same cycle.

Mortality Themes

- Sudden parental death
- Childhood grief and loss of safety
- Nature as teacher and mirror of mortality
- Coming of age through loss
- Resilience and continuity of life

Discussion Prompts

1. How does the film portray grief without using explicit language about death?

2. Why do you think Bambi's father is emotionally distant rather than comforting?

3. How does the forest itself function as a character in the story?

4. What lessons does Bambi learn about survival, responsibility, and leadership after his mother's death?

5. How might this film shape a child's first understanding of loss?

6. How does the film's lack of adult explanation place the viewer in the same emotional position as Bambi?

Movie Pairings and Activities

- Pair the movie with *The Lion King* (1994) to compare depictions of parental death and leadership.

- Or pair it with *Finding Nemo* (2003) to explore how loss shapes parenting and fear.

- Invite viewers to reflect on their first memory of loss and how it changed their sense of safety.

- Discuss how animals are often used in storytelling to make difficult topics more approachable.

Final Thought

Bambi endures not because it explains death but because it honors grief quietly. The forest does not stop, the seasons continue, and life moves forward, carrying loss within it rather than around it. For many viewers, this film plants the first seed of an essential truth: Love makes us vulnerable, and growth often begins where innocence ends.

Big Hero 6 *(2014, PG, 1 h 42 min)*

Starring: (voices) Ryan Potter, Scott Adsit, Jamie Chung, Damon Wayans Jr., Maya Rudolph

Directed by: Don Hall and Chris Williams

Film Description

Teen prodigy Hiro Hamada's world is shattered when his older brother Tadashi dies in a sudden fire. Tadashi's greatest creation, Baymax, a gentle inflatable healthcare robot, becomes Hiro's unexpected companion in grief. Consumed by anger and guilt, Hiro initially reprograms Baymax into a tool for revenge. But Baymax's core directive is healing, not harm. As Hiro confronts his pain, he learns that honoring his brother's legacy means choosing compassion over destruction and connection over isolation.

Mortality Themes

- Sudden sibling loss
- Grief expressed as anger and revenge
- Legacy carried forward through creation
- Healing as both emotional and physical
- Choosing meaning after loss

Discussion Prompts

1. How does Hiro's grief show up in his behavior and decision-making?
2. In what ways does Baymax function as a stand-in for Tadashi's continued care and presence?
3. Why is revenge such a tempting response to grief in this story?
4. What does the film suggest about how we honor those who have died?
5. How does healing differ from forgetting in Hiro's journey?
6. How does the film portray the difference between honoring someone's memory and being driven by unresolved grief?

Movie Pairings and Activities

- Pair the movie with *Finding Nemo* (2003) to explore how loss reshapes motivation and fear.
- Or pair it with *Inside Out* (2015) to discuss emotions as signals rather than problems to fix.
- Invite viewers to identify a healthy outlet they have used, or could use, for grief-fueled anger.
- Discuss the idea of legacy beyond physical inheritance, such as values, care, or creativity.

Final Thought

Big Hero 6 reminds us that grief does not ask to be erased but transformed. Baymax embodies a radical message: Pain deserves care, not suppression or retaliation. In choosing healing over vengeance, Hiro discovers that love does not end with death; it simply changes shape and waits to be carried forward.

The Book of Life *(2014, PG, 1 h 35 min)*

Starring: (voices) Diego Luna, Zoe Saldana, Channing Tatum, Ron Perlman

Directed by: Jorge R. Gutierrez

Film Description

Manolo is a gentle music-loving young man caught between honoring his family's long tradition of bullfighting and following his own artistic heart. When a wager between supernatural forces sends him on an unexpected journey through multiple realms of the afterlife, Manolo must confront fear, love, loyalty, and his own mortality. Along the way, he learns that courage is not measured by violence or bravado but by authenticity, compassion, and remembrance. The film presents the afterlife not as a static endpoint but as a vibrant continuation shaped by memory, love, and legacy.

Mortality Themes

- Afterlife as a living, evolving realm
- Memory as a source of identity after death
- Love that transcends death
- Living authentically in the face of mortality
- Family traditions, remembrance, and cultural legacy
- The acceptance of death as part of life

Discussion Prompts

1. How does the film portray afterlife differently from the more traditional depictions?

2. What role does memory play in keeping the dead present in the world of the living?

3. In what ways is Manolo's greatest struggle about living fully rather than fearing death?

4. How do family expectations shape the choices we make about our lives and values?

5. What does the film suggest about bravery, and how does that connect to mortality?

6. How does the film use celebration and color to reduce fear around death without minimizing its importance?

Movie Pairings and Activities

- Pair the film with *Coco* (2017) to explore the cultural traditions surrounding remembrance and afterlife.

- Or pair it with *The Lion King* (1994) to discuss legacy, ancestors, and the guidance of those who came before us.

- Invite viewers to share a story about a loved one who lives on through family traditions or memories.

- Discuss how cultural rituals help people integrate death into everyday life.

Final Thought

The Book of Life offers a joyful reminder that death does not erase us; instead, it reframes what matters the most while we are alive. Through music, color, and myth, the film gently teaches that the truest way to honor the dead is to live honestly, love boldly, and remember well.

Coco *(2017, PG, 1 h 45 min)*

Starring: (voices) Anthony Gonzalez, Gael García Bernal, Benjamin Bratt, Alanna Ubach

Directed by: Lee Unkrich and Adrian Molina

Film Description

Miguel is a young boy who dreams of becoming a musician despite his family's long-standing ban on music. On *Día de los Muertos*, a mysterious chain of events transports him to the Land of the Dead where he searches for his great-great-grandfather, a legendary musician he believes can help him return home. Along the way, Miguel uncovers family secrets, confronts painful misunderstandings, and learns that love, memory, and forgiveness can bridge even the divide between life and death. The film beautifully weaves cultural tradition, humor, and emotional depth into a story that honors both ancestors and the living.

Mortality Themes

- Remembrance as a way of keeping the dead alive
- Cultural rituals surrounding death and honoring ancestors
- Generational wounds and reconciliation
- Identity shaped by family history
- The fear of being forgotten after death
- Love and forgiveness as healing forces across generations

Discussion Prompts

1. How does the film portray death as a continuation of relationship rather than an ending?
2. What happens in the Land of the Dead when people are no longer remembered, and what does that suggest about legacy?
3. How do misunderstandings between generations shape family stories and identities?
4. In what ways do rituals like *Día de los Muertos* help the living process grief?
5. How does Miguel's journey reflect the balance between honoring family tradition and following personal passion?
6. How does the fear of being forgotten influence behavior both in the Land of the Dead and among the living?

Movie Pairings and Activities

- Pair the film with *The Book of Life* (2014) to explore the cultural approaches to afterlife and remembrance.
- Or pair it with *Up* (2009) to discuss memory, loss, and continuing bonds.
- Invite viewers to create a small remembrance activity such as sharing stories or photos of loved ones.

- Discuss how different cultures honor ancestors and what rituals feel meaningful today.

Final Thought

Coco reminds us that death does not end our relationships. It challenges the idea that forgetting is inevitable and instead celebrates memory as a living act of love. Through music, color, and storytelling, the film gently teaches that, when we remember well, we keep each other alive in the ways that matter the most.

Corpse Bride *(2005, PG, 1 h 17 min)*

Starring: (voices) Johnny Depp, Helena Bonham Carter, Emily Watson

Directed by: Tim Burton and Mike Johnson

Film Description

Victor Van Dort is a shy young man nervously rehearsing his wedding vows in the forest when he accidentally places the ring on what turns out to be the finger of a deceased bride. Emily, the Corpse Bride, rises from the grave believing she has finally been married and whisks Victor away to the Land of the Dead. What follows is a visually rich, darkly whimsical journey between the world of the living and the afterlife where Victor must confront duty, love, and choice. The afterlife is lively, colorful, and full of personality, while the land of the living appears rigid and gray. Beneath its gothic charm, the story gently explores grief, justice, and the possibility of release after death.

Mortality Themes

- A vibrant and relational vision of the afterlife
- Love beyond death and the necessity of letting go
- Justice and unfinished business after dying
- The contrast between emotional vitality and emotional repression
- The acceptance of death as a transition rather than a punishment
- Honoring truth and autonomy, even beyond the grave

Discussion Prompts

1. How does the film's depiction of afterlife differ from the traditional portrayals of death as dark or frightening?

2. Why do you think the Land of the Dead feels more alive than the world of the living?

3. What unfinished business keeps Emily tied to the living world, and how is it resolved?

4. How does the story balance romantic love with the necessity of release and closure?

5. What does the film suggest about choice and consent, both in life and after death?

6. What does the film suggest about emotional truth versus social obligation when it comes to love, marriage, and death?

Movie Pairings and Activities

- Pair the movie with *Beetlejuice* (1988) to compare playful afterlife worlds and tone.

- Or pair it with *Ghost* (1990) to discuss unfinished business and love after death.

- Invite discussion about what makes a "good death" in storytelling versus real life.

- Explore how animation can safely introduce death-related themes to younger audiences.

Final Thought

Corpse Bride offers a surprisingly tender meditation on death, reminding us that love does not mean possession and that true devotion sometimes requires letting go. With humor, music, and heart, the film suggests that peace after death comes not from clinging to what was lost but from releasing it with honesty and grace.

Finding Nemo *(2003, G, 1 h 30 min)*

Starring: (voices) Albert Brooks, Ellen DeGeneres, Alexander Gould

Directed by: Andrew Stanton

Film Description

Finding Nemo begins with a sudden and devastating loss. Marlin, a clownfish, survives a barracuda attack that kills his mate Coral and all but one of their eggs. Traumatized by this event, Marlin becomes an intensely anxious and overprotective single father to his son, Nemo. When Nemo is captured by a diver and taken far from home, Marlin is forced into an epic journey across the ocean to rescue him. Along the way, he encounters danger, unlikely allies, and his own deepest fears. The film gently but clearly shows how unresolved grief can shape parenting, relationships, and identity and how healing often requires risk, trust, and connection.

Mortality Themes

- Sudden death and traumatic loss
- Parental grief and fear-based protection
- Living in the shadow of mortality
- Resilience and renewal after loss
- Letting go as an act of love
- Trust, growth, and acceptance of uncertainty

Discussion Prompts

1. How does the death of Coral influence Marlin's behavior throughout the film?

2. When does protection become fear, and how does fear limit living fully?

3. What lessons does Marlin learn about trust and letting go by the end of the story?

4. How does the film portray resilience without minimizing grief?

5. Why do you think this story resonates so strongly with both children and adults?

6. How does the film distinguish between keeping a child safe and preparing them to live independently?

Movie Pairings and Activities

- Pair the movie with *Bambi* (1942) to compare portrayals of parental loss in animated films.

- Or pair it with *Up* (2009) to discuss how grief can initially shrink a life and later expand it.

- Use the film as a conversation starter with families about fear, safety, and independence.

- Invite viewers to reflect on how loss has shaped their own risk tolerance in life.

Final Thought

Finding Nemo reminds us that love, when guided by fear, can unintentionally limit the very lives we are trying to protect. Through humor, adventure, and heart, the film offers a powerful message: Honoring those we have lost does not mean avoiding risk forever. It means learning how to live, love, and trust again in a world where loss is possible, but joy still waits just beyond the reef.

Inside Out *(2015, PG, 1 h 35 min)*

Starring: (voices) Amy Poehler, Phyllis Smith, Bill Hader, Lewis Black, Mindy Kaling

Directed by: Pete Docter

Film Description

Inside Out takes place largely inside the mind of eleven-year-old Riley where five core emotions Joy, Sadness, Fear, Anger, and Disgust work together to help her navigate daily life. When Riley's family moves from the Midwest to San Francisco, her familiar world disappears almost overnight. The upheaval triggers emotional chaos inside her mind, especially as Joy tries desperately to keep Riley happy while pushing Sadness aside. As Joy and Sadness become lost within Riley's inner landscape, Riley begins to emotionally shut down. The story ultimately reveals that grief, sadness, and loss are not obstacles to happiness but essential parts of emotional healing and growth.

Mortality Themes

- Loss of place, identity, and childhood security
- Emotional grief without physical death
- The necessity of sadness in healing
- Emotional honesty as a path to resilience
- Growing up as a series of small deaths and transformations
- Integrating joy and sorrow as part of living fully

Discussion Prompts

1. How does Riley's move represent a form of grief even though no one has died?
2. Why does Joy resist Sadness, and what does she learn by the end of the film?
3. How does the film challenge the idea that happiness should be the goal at all times?
4. In what ways does *Inside Out* normalize sadness as a healthy emotional response?
5. How might this film help children and adults talk about grief more openly?
6. How might suppressing sadness actually delay healing after a loss or major change?

Movie Pairings and Activities

- Pair the film with *Up* (2009) to explore how loss shapes identity and emotional growth.
- Or pair it with *Bambi* (1942) to compare early-life grief experiences in animated films.

- Use the film as a tool for discussing emotional literacy with children or families.
- Invite viewers to name and reflect on emotions they avoid during times of loss.

Final Thought

Inside Out gently but powerfully teaches that sadness is not a problem to be fixed but a truth to be honored. By giving grief a voice and a purpose, the film helps audiences of all ages understand that healing does not come from denying pain but from allowing it to be seen, shared, and integrated. In doing so, *Inside Out* offers one of the clearest animated lessons: that living fully requires making room for sorrow right alongside joy.

The Lady and the Reaper *(2009, TV-G, 8 min)*

Starring: (Animated short, no voice cast listed)

Directed by: Javier Recio Gracia

Film Description

This darkly comic animated short opens with an elderly woman living alone, quietly longing to be reunited with her late husband. When the Grim Reaper finally arrives to escort her to death, the moment feels peaceful and welcome. That serenity is quickly disrupted when aggressive modern medical interventions repeatedly yank her back from death's doorstep. What follows is a fast-paced slapstick battle between Death and modern medicine, with the woman caught in the middle. Though humorous on the surface, the film raises pointed questions about dignity, autonomy, and whether prolonging life at all costs truly serves the person who is dying.

Mortality Themes

- Acceptance of death as a natural transition
- Desire for reunion after death
- Medical overreach at the end of life
- Autonomy versus intervention

- Quality of life versus life prolongation
- Humor as a lens for difficult truths

Discussion Prompts

1. How does the woman's attitude toward death contrast with the medical response to her condition?

2. What does the film suggest about intention versus outcome in end-of-life care?

3. How does humor make the film's critique of medical intervention more accessible?

4. In what ways does the Grim Reaper function as a compassionate figure rather than a frightening one?

5. How might this short spark conversations about advance directives and personal wishes?

6. What ethical tensions arise when medical capability conflicts with a person's clearly expressed wishes?

Movie Pairings and Activities

- Pair the film with *Wit* (2001) to compare medical intervention and patient dignity.
- Or pair it with *Soul* (2020) to contrast playful and philosophical approaches to death.
- Use the film as a short discussion starter before longer films about end-of-life care.
- Invite viewers to reflect on what a "good death" might mean to them.

Final Thought

In just eight minutes, *The Lady and the Reaper* delivers a surprisingly sharp meditation on death with wit, warmth, and visual flair. By framing end-of-life struggles through comedy, the film invites audiences to laugh first and then think deeply about dignity, timing, and listening to what the dying may already know. It reminds us that, sometimes, the most compassionate act is not fighting death but honoring the life that has already been fully lived.

The Lion King *(1994, G, 1 h 28 min)*

Starring: (voices) Matthew Broderick, James Earl Jones, Jeremy Irons, Moira Kelly, Nathan Lane, Ernie Sabella, Whoopi Goldberg

Directed by: Roger Allers and Rob Minkoff

Music by: Elton John and Tim Rice

Film Description

This landmark Disney animated film follows young lion prince Simba whose carefree childhood is shattered by the sudden and traumatic death of his father, King Mufasa. Manipulated by his uncle Scar, Simba believes he is responsible for the tragedy and flees his homeland in shame. As he grows up in exile, Simba adopts a philosophy of avoidance and emotional numbing until he is called back to confront his past, reclaim his identity, and take his place in the circle of life. While wrapped in vibrant animation and memorable music, the story offers a surprisingly direct and enduring portrayal of grief, guilt, and the journey toward healing.

Mortality Themes

- Parental death and childhood bereavement
- Survivor guilt and self-blame
- Disenfranchised grief and emotional avoidance
- Continuing bonds with the dead
- Identity formation after loss
- Acceptance of death as part of the circle of life

Discussion Prompts

1. How does Simba's response to Mufasa's death reflect common grief reactions in children?
2. What role does guilt play in Simba's exile and emotional shutdown?
3. How do different characters model contrasting approaches to grief and remembrance?

4. What does the circle-of-life philosophy suggest about death and continuity?

5. How does Simba's reconnection with his father's memory support his healing?

6. How does the film model the difference between remembering with love and being trapped by guilt?

Movie Pairings and Activities

- Pair the movie with *Bambi* (1942) to compare portrayals of parental death in animated films.

- Or pair it with *Coco* (2017) to explore continuing bonds across generations.

- Invite viewers to discuss childhood memories of encountering death through film.

- Use the film to open conversations about grief with children and families.

Final Thought

The Lion King endures because it speaks honestly to loss while offering hope without minimizing pain. Through Simba's journey, the film affirms that grief does not disappear when ignored and that healing often requires returning to what hurts the most. By honoring the dead, accepting responsibility without shame, and embracing connection, the story reminds us that love continues even after death and that remembering can be a powerful act of courage.

Soul *(2020, PG, 1 h 40 min)*

Starring: (voices) Jamie Foxx, Tina Fey, Angela Bassett, Phylicia Rashad, Questlove

Directed by: Pete Docter and Kemp Powers

Film Description

Joe Gardner is a middle-school band teacher who dreams of becoming a professional jazz musician. Just as his long-awaited big break finally arrives, he suffers a sudden accident that launches him into a metaphysical realm between life and death. Determined not to die before he has truly lived, Joe navigates the Great Before, a playful yet profound space where souls develop personalities before heading to Earth. Along the way, he mentors a skeptical soul named 22 and begins to question his long-held belief that life's value lies in achievement rather than experience. What unfolds is a deeply thoughtful meditation on purpose, presence, and what it really means to be alive.

Mortality Themes

- Near-death experiences and liminal spaces
- Fear of a wasted life
- Purpose versus presence
- The meaning of legacy beyond accomplishment
- Existential anxiety and fulfillment
- Living fully in ordinary moments

Discussion Prompts

1. How does Joe define a "life well lived" at the beginning of the film, and how does that change?
2. What does the film suggest about purpose versus passion?
3. How does *Soul* challenge the traditional ideas of legacy and success?
4. What moments in the film highlight the importance of everyday experiences?
5. How might this story resonate differently with adults than with children?
6. How does the film challenge the idea that one defining purpose gives life its value?

Movie Pairings and Activities

- Pair the movie with *Inside Out* (2015) to explore emotional and existential development.
- Or pair it with *It's a Wonderful Life* (1946) to compare reckonings with life's meaning.

- Invite viewers to reflect on moments when they felt the most alive even if nothing "important" happened.

- Use the film as a prompt for journaling about purpose, joy, and overlooked blessings.

Final Thought

Soul gently reminds us that life is not something we earn through greatness but something we inhabit through attention. By reframing legacy as the quiet influence we have on others rather than the milestones we achieve, the film offers a compassionate antidote to fear-driven living. It whispers a simple truth: Meaning is not found in chasing sparks but in noticing them when they appear.

Up *(2009, PG, 1 h 36 min)*

Starring: (voices) Ed Asner, Jordan Nagai, Christopher Plummer

Directed by: Pete Docter and Bob Peterson

Film Description

Up opens with one of the most emotionally resonant montages in animation history, chronicling the lifelong love between Carl and Ellie Fredricksen. When Ellie dies, Carl becomes a reclusive widower, clinging tightly to their shared home and memories. Determined to fulfill the adventure they once dreamed of, Carl lifts his house with thousands of balloons and sets off for South America. Along the way, he unexpectedly forms new relationships with a young boy scout named Russell, a rare bird, and a loyal dog. What begins as an escape from grief becomes a journey toward connection, healing, and the realization that new adventures do not erase old love.

Mortality Themes

- Spousal loss and continuing bonds

- Grief expressed through withdrawal and rigidity

- Aging, regret, and unfinished dreams

- The tension between holding on and letting go

- Healing through unexpected relationships
- Reengaging with life after loss

Discussion Prompts

1. How does the opening montage shape our understanding of Carl's grief?

2. In what ways does Carl's house symbolize his relationship with Ellie and his resistance to change?

3. How does *Up* portray continuing bonds rather than "moving on" from grief?

4. What role do Russell and the other companions play in Carl's healing?

5. How does the film redefine what counts as an "adventure"?

6. What helps Carl shift from preserving the past to making space for the present?

Movie Pairings and Activities

- Pair the film with *A Man Called Otto* (2022) to explore grief, aging, and reengagement with life.

- Or pair it with *Finding Nemo* (2003) to examine how fear after loss can shape behavior.

- Invite viewers to reflect on what emotional "baggage" they may be carrying and what they might be ready to release.

- Encourage discussion about honoring the dead while still saying yes to new connections.

Final Thought

Up gently teaches that grief is not something to conquer but something to carry wisely. Carl does not betray Ellie by opening his heart again; he honors her by continuing to live. The film offers a hopeful truth for mourners of all ages: Love does not end with death, and life still has room for surprise, tenderness, and joy.

Animated Films: Closing Thoughts

Animated films remind us that mortality does not require grimness to be taken seriously. Through humor, beauty, and imagination, they show us that grief can coexist with joy, memory with movement, and endings with beginnings. These stories give us permission to feel deeply, to ask questions, and to talk about death without fear.

If a cartoon can help a child understand sadness or help an adult remember how to hope again, then animation has done sacred work. These films show us that, even when words fail, stories still know how to speak. And sometimes, they sing.

As educators, caregivers, or simply fellow travelers on this mortal ride, we can use animated films to open gentle doorways into conversations that matter. And as viewers, we're reminded that, no matter our age, we're all still learning how to live, how to love, and how to let go.

Animated films may be drawn, but the lessons they offer are deeply, beautifully real.

ESTATE PLANNING

Introduction

Estate planning rarely makes the list of things people *want* to think about. It feels dry, technical, and safely ignorable, until it isn't. These films step into that uncomfortable gap between "someday" and "too late," showing what happens when plans are made, ignored, misunderstood, or left entirely undone.

Rather than focusing solely on legal documents, the movies in this chapter explore the human side of planning. They reveal how wills, insurance, property, and final wishes can either protect the people we love or unintentionally burden them. Some stories unfold with humor, others with heartbreak, but all of them remind us that estate planning is less about stuff and more about stewardship, responsibility, and care.

By watching these characters navigate inheritances, housing, caregiving, and unfinished business, we are invited to reflect on our own preparations. These films give us permission to ask hard questions in a gentler way, using stories as a bridge between avoidance and action.

Being There *(1979, PG, 2 h 10 min)*

Starring: Peter Sellers, Shirley MacLaine, Melvyn Douglas

Directed by: Hal Ashby

Film Description

Chance is a gentle, simple-minded gardener who has spent his entire life living quietly in a Washington, DC, townhouse, tending plants and watching television. When the wealthy man who owns the home dies, Chance is abruptly turned out with no plan, no legal protection, and no understanding of how the world works. Dressed impeccably but utterly unprepared, he wanders into the lives of powerful political and financial elites who mistake his literal garden-based observations for profound wisdom.

Chance's accidental rise exposes how easily meaning, authority, and intelligence can be projected onto someone who fits the right image. Beneath the satire, the film quietly raises practical estate planning questions: Who is responsible for a dependent adult? What happens when someone dies without clear plans? How much power do appearances and assumptions hold when legal structures fail to protect the vulnerable?

Mortality Themes

- Absence of estate planning and unintended consequences
- Care planning for cognitively impaired or dependent adults
- Power, wealth, and who controls decisions at the end of life
- How meaning and authority are projected after death
- The vulnerability created by silence, secrecy, or neglect

Discussion Prompts

1. What happens to Chance because no plans were made for his care after the homeowner's death?

2. How might the story have changed if legal guardianship or instructions had been in place?

3. What does the film suggest about how society confuses appearance with competence or authority?

4. In what ways does television shape how characters perceive reality, power, and truth?

5. How does Chance's vulnerability highlight ethical responsibilities around care planning, not just asset distribution?

6. Chance's presence allows Ben Rand to relax about his impending death. Have you seen how specific people make a positive influence when a loved one is dying?

Movie Pairings and Activities

- Pair the film with *The Six Wives of Henry Lefay* (2009) to contrast intentional planning with chaos.

- Or pair it with *About Schmidt* (2002) for another look at legacy, control, and late-life decisions.

- Draft a basic letter of instruction outlining care wishes for a dependent loved one.

- Discuss about who would speak for you if you could not speak for yourself.

Final Thought

Being There reminds us that estate planning is not just about money; it is about responsibility, protection, and dignity. When plans are not made, others will fill in the gaps, sometimes wisely, sometimes dangerously. Chance survives because he is lucky, not because anyone planned for him. The film gently but firmly suggests that leaving life decisions to chance is rarely an act of kindness, even when the garden looks peaceful.

The Ghost and Mrs. Muir *(1947, PG, 1h 47 min)*

Starring: Gene Tierney, Rex Harrison

Directed by: Joseph L. Mankiewicz

Film Description

Lucy Muir is a young widow at the turn of the twentieth century determined to live life on her own terms. Defying her in-laws and social expectations, she rents a seaside cottage only to discover it is haunted by the blunt, opinionated ghost of its former owner, Captain Daniel Gregg. The captain died suddenly and, inconveniently, without a will. While his ghost fiercely resists change, Lucy gradually builds a life in the home, guided by her independence, creativity, and quiet resilience.

Through a touch of Hollywood magic, Lucy collaborates with the ghost to write his life story. The book becomes a bestseller, providing her with financial security, the ability to purchase the home outright, and the freedom to make thoughtful estate plans of her own. Beneath the romance and supernatural charm lies a surprisingly practical story about autonomy, property rights, legacy, and how unfinished planning can echo long after death.

Mortality Themes

- Dying without a will and unintended consequences
- Property ownership and women's financial independence
- Autonomy in life and clarity in death
- Legacy creation through storytelling
- Continuing bonds and love beyond the grave

Discussion Prompts

1. How does Captain Gregg's lack of a will affect what happens to his home and legacy?
2. In what ways does Lucy's financial independence allow her greater control over her life and future planning?
3. How does the film portray autonomy differently for men and women in the 1940s?
4. What does legacy mean in this story: property, money, memory, or love?
5. How does Captain Gregg's resistance to planning mirror common attitudes toward death avoidance?
6. What aspects of Lucy's story still feel relevant to financial and housing independence today?

Movie Pairings and Activities

- Pair the movie with *Being There* (1979) to contrast accidental outcomes with intentional planning.
- Or pair it with *The Last Word* (2017) for another take on shaping one's legacy before death.
- Write a short "letter of intent" explaining what matters the most to you about your home or possessions.

- If your house could talk, discuss what it would say about how you lived.

Final Thought

At heart, *The Ghost and Mrs. Muir* is a gentle reminder that love may linger but legal clarity does not magically appear after death. Captain Gregg's line, "I didn't leave a will," because he didn't plan to die, lands as a cautionary truth. Lucy's story shows how intention, planning, and self-determination can turn uncertainty into security. The film leaves us with a comforting notion: Love may transcend death, but a good estate plan makes life much easier for everyone still standing on the shore.

The Grand Budapest Hotel *(2014, R, 1 h 39 min)*

Starring: Ralph Fiennes, F. Murray Abraham, Tony Revolori, Saoirse Ronan, Tilda Swinton, Adrien Brody, Willem Dafoe

Directed by: Wes Anderson

Film Description

Presented as a story within a story within a story, *The Grand Budapest Hotel* follows the life of Gustave H., a meticulously mannered concierge at a once-glorious European hotel, and Zero, his devoted protégé. When one of Gustave's wealthy lovers dies under suspicious circumstances, he unexpectedly becomes the primary heir to a priceless Renaissance painting. Her family is not amused.

What follows is a whirlwind of accusations, imprisonments, murders, narrow escapes, and exquisitely framed chaos. Beneath the pastel colors and dry humor lies a sharp examination of inheritance disputes, unchecked greed, and how death can bring out both the best and the worst in people. The hotel itself becomes a metaphor for legacy, memory, and what happens when stories are preserved or lost over time.

Mortality Themes

- Inheritance disputes and contested wills
- Greed and entitlement after death

- Death as a catalyst for revealing character
- Preservation of legacy through memory and storytelling
- The fragility of cultural and personal history

Discussion Prompts

1. How does the absence or ambiguity of clear estate planning escalate conflict in the story?

2. What does the painting represent beyond monetary value?

3. In what ways does the film suggest that legacy is about more than possessions?

4. How does humor function as a coping mechanism in the face of death and betrayal?

5. How does the film portray the difference between entitlement and stewardship when wealth is involved?

6. What role does clear documentation play in preventing the kind of chaos depicted in the story?

Movie Pairings and Activities

- Pair the movie with *Knives Out* (2019) for another darkly comic look at inheritance and family dysfunction.

- Or pair it with *Being There* (1979) to compare perceived wisdom versus actual planning.

- Discuss which personal items might cause conflict if left unspecified.

- Write about a nonmonetary legacy you would want remembered about you.

Final Thought

The Grand Budapest Hotel reminds us that, when the destiny of a great fortune is at stake, clarity matters. Without thoughtful estate planning, grief can quickly curdle into conflict, and love can be overshadowed by entitlement. Wrapped in whimsy and razor-sharp humor, the film offers a sly but serious lesson: Stories endure best when intentions are clear, and legacies are shaped with care rather than left to chance.

Places in the Heart *(1984, PG, 1 h 51 min)*

Starring: Sally Field, Danny Glover, John Malkovich, Ed Harris

Directed by: Robert Benton

Film Description

Set during the Great Depression, *Places in the Heart* begins with a sudden tragedy when Edna Spalding's husband is accidentally killed, leaving her widowed with two young children and a struggling farm in rural Texas. With no insurance, mounting debt, and a mortgage due, Edna must quickly adapt or lose everything.

What follows is not just a survival story but a portrait of resilience. Edna forms an unlikely household that includes a blind boarder and a Black farmhand, creating a chosen family bound by necessity and shared humanity. The film quietly portrays how death once unfolded in the home, with the deceased laid out on the dining room table, and how practical realities often leave little room for prolonged mourning.

Mortality Themes

- Sudden death and unprepared families
- Financial vulnerability after loss
- Lack of insurance and estate planning consequences
- Grief as a catalyst for resilience
- Chosen family and community support
- Faith, forgiveness, and endurance

Discussion Prompts

1. How does the absence of financial and estate planning shape Edna's options after her husband's death?
2. What systems, formal or informal, help Edna survive her loss?
3. How does grief operate quietly in this film rather than overtly?
4. What does the film suggest about dignity in death and survival in life?

5. How might Edna's experience differ if even minimal planning or insurance had been in place?

6. What does the film suggest about the limits of self-reliance after loss?

Movie Pairings and Activities

- Pair the film with *Ordinary People* (1980) to contrast private versus communal grief.

- Or pair it with *The Straight Story* (1999) for quiet resilience in the face of hardship.

- Discuss what financial protections families rely on today that were absent in the 1930s.

- Reflect on who would step in if your household structure suddenly changed.

Final Thought

Places in the Heart is a gentle but powerful reminder that death does not pause the practical demands of living. When loss arrives without preparation, survivors are forced to improvise, adapt, and lean on community. The film honors quiet courage and shows that estate planning is not just about assets but about protecting the people who must keep going when everything changes overnight.

Estate Planning: Closing Thoughts

If these films teach us anything, it's that estate planning is an act of love, not a morbid chore. The absence of a plan rarely creates freedom. More often, it creates confusion, conflict, and unnecessary suffering for the people left behind. A thoughtful plan, on the other hand, can offer clarity, dignity, and peace during an already difficult time.

These stories also remind us that no plan is purely technical. Documents reflect values. Choices reveal priorities. Whether through humor, tragedy, or quiet realism, these films show how preparation can protect relationships and preserve meaning long after someone is gone.

If you finish this chapter feeling nudged to update a will, review beneficiaries, or start a conversation you've been avoiding, consider that a successful viewing experience. Estate planning is not about predicting the future; it's about caring for the people who will have to live in it.

HARD-TO-CATEGORIZE MORTALITY MOVIES

Introduction

Some films slip neatly into categories. Others refuse to behave.

The movies in this chapter don't announce themselves as Mortality Movies, yet death, dying, loss, or impermanence quietly (or not so quietly) shape their stories. In some, mortality arrives sideways through satire, absurdity, or genre play. In others, it shows up unexpectedly, altering the emotional gravity of what might otherwise look like comedy, romance, or adventure.

These films are difficult to label precisely because they mirror real life. Death rarely arrives on schedule or in the expected form. It interrupts road trips, derails family plans, exposes denial, deepens love, and sometimes even becomes a punchline. These stories remind us that mortality is not confined to hospital rooms or funerals. It weaves through everyday life, shaping our choices, our relationships, and our capacity for meaning.

This chapter invites curiosity. Watch for the moments where laughter catches in your throat, where a seemingly minor death reframes the entire story, or where characters reveal more about living by the way they respond to loss. These films may be hard to categorize, but they are rich conversation starters.

After.Life *(2009, R, 1 h 44 min)*

Starring: Christina Ricci, Liam Neeson, Justin Long

Directed by: Agnieszka Wojtowicz-Vosloo

Film Description

After a devastating car accident, Anna Taylor awakens on a slab in a funeral home preparation room. Funeral director Eliot Deacon calmly informs her that she is dead and begins preparing her body for burial. Anna insists she is alive, frightened, confused, and pleading to be released. As the film unfolds, viewers are pulled into a psychological maze where reality, perception, trauma, and control blur together. Is Anna truly dead, or is she trapped in a living nightmare constructed by someone who holds absolute authority over her fate?

The story keeps us uncomfortably suspended between possibilities, forcing us to question what defines death, who gets to declare it, and how power operates in moments when a person is the most vulnerable. And because it portrays a funeral director in a very creepy light, the film is listed here rather than at the very start of the funeral director film section.

Mortality Themes

- The ambiguity of death and dying
- Fear of premature death and being buried alive
- Power dynamics between professionals and the vulnerable
- Loss of bodily autonomy
- Psychological death versus physical death

Discussion Prompts

1. What signals do you rely on to define whether someone is alive or dead?

2. How much authority should medical or death-care professionals hold over determining death?

3. In what ways does fear distort Anna's perception of reality, and how might trauma play a role?

4. How does the film challenge our trust in institutions meant to care for us at the end of life?

5. What does this story suggest about the difference between being alive and truly living?

6. How might this film change the way viewers think about trust, consent, and vulnerability at the end of life?

Movie Pairings and Activities

- Pair the movie with *Jacob's Ladder* (1990) for another unsettling exploration of the liminal states between life and death.

- Or pair it with *Wit* (2001) to contrast compassionate versus dehumanizing encounters around mortality.

- Discuss advance directives and how they protect autonomy when a person cannot speak for themselves.

- Explore cultural and medical definitions of death across time and societies.

Final Thought

After.Life unsettles because it taps into a primal fear: losing control at the very moment our lives matter the most. Whether interpreted as a psychological thriller, a social commentary, or an existential parable, the film reminds us how essential clarity, consent, and compassion are when navigating the fragile boundary between life and death.

Chocolat *(2000, PG-13, 2 h 1 min)*

Starring: Juliette Binoche, Judi Dench, Johnny Depp, Alfred Molina

Directed by: Lasse Hallström

Film Description

Set in a conservative French village during the winter of 1959, *Chocolat* follows Vianne Rocher, a free-spirited single mother, who arrives with her young daughter and opens a chocolate shop directly across from the church during Lent. Her presence disrupts the town's rigid traditions and unspoken rules, stirring long-buried desires, grief, and secrets among the villagers.

At the heart of the story is Armande Voizin, an elderly woman estranged from her daughter and denied contact with her grandson. As Armande reconnects with joy, pleasure, and agency late in life, she makes deliberate choices about how she wants to live and die. The film quietly but powerfully explores how embracing life can also mean making peace with death.

One of *Chocolat*'s subtle mortality threads is Vianne's relationship with her deceased mother. She carries her mother's ashes everywhere in a small urn, a literal and symbolic burden. Her mother warned her never to settle down, framing rootedness as a kind of danger or curse. As a result, Vianne lives in perpetual motion, unable to put down roots or fully belong.

The turning point comes when the urn breaks and the ashes are scattered. This moment releases Vianne from inherited fear and unresolved grief. It's a powerful metaphor for continuing bonds gone awry. When remembrance becomes obligation rather than love, it can trap the living.

Only after the ashes are released does Vianne choose to stay, to belong, and to risk connection. The film quietly suggests that grief passed down unexamined can dictate our lives and that healing may involve letting the dead rest, loosening their grip on our choices.

Mortality Themes

- Living fully in the face of mortality
- Honoring final wishes and personal autonomy
- Reconciliation and unresolved family grief
- Aging, illness, and chosen joy at the end of life
- Cultural and religious attitudes toward pleasure and death

Discussion Prompts

1. How does Armande define a "good death," and how does it differ from her family's expectations?

2. In what ways does the town's fear of pleasure mirror its discomfort with death?

3. How does food function as a metaphor for life, memory, and connection in the film?

4. What does the story suggest about agency at the end of life, especially for elders?

5. How do unspoken family conflicts complicate grief before and after death?

6. How does the scattering of Vianne's mother's ashes redefine the difference between remembrance and release?

Movie Pairings and Activities

- Pair the movie with *Harold and Maude* (1971) to explore unconventional approaches to living and dying well.

- Or pair it with *Steel Magnolias* (1989) for stories where community softens loss.

- Invite viewers to reflect on what brings them joy now and what they hope to still enjoy late in life.

- Discuss how final wishes are shaped by culture, religion, and family dynamics.

Final Thought

Chocolat reminds us that preparing for death is inseparable from learning how to live. By savoring pleasure, choosing connection, and releasing old resentments, the film suggests that a life fully tasted leaves fewer regrets when the end arrives.

Don't Look Up *(2021, R, 2 h 18 min)*

Starring: Leonardo DiCaprio, Jennifer Lawrence, Meryl Streep, Jonah Hill, Mark Rylance

Directed by: Adam McKay

Film Description

In this sharp-edged satire, two astronomers discover a planet-killing comet on a direct collision course with Earth. With only six months before total extinction, they attempt to warn the public, politicians, and media outlets. Their scientifically sound message is met with indifference, distraction, spin, and outright denial.

As the clock ticks down, society continues to prioritize profit, entertainment, and personal comfort over collective survival. The looming certainty of death becomes background noise, reduced to hashtags, memes, and partisan talking points. Rather than mobilizing in the face of shared mortality, humanity fractures into camps of belief, disbelief, and willful ignorance.

Mortality Themes

- Collective denial of death and extinction
- Fear avoidance and distraction as coping mechanisms
- Power, profit, and control at the end of life
- Individual versus communal responsibility
- How societies respond when death is unavoidable

Discussion Prompts

1. Why is widespread denial such a common response to existential threats?
2. How does humor function as both a coping tool and a form of avoidance in the film?
3. What parallels can be drawn between the comet and how we approach personal mortality?
4. Who benefits from denial, and who pays the price?
5. How might honest conversations about death change collective decision-making?
6. If the characters had fully accepted the comet's certainty earlier, what different ethical or emotion choices might have emerged?

Movie Pairings and Activities

- Pair the film with *Dr. Strangelove* (1964) for satirical takes on global annihilation.

- Or pair it with *The Seventh Seal* (1957) to contrast intimate versus societal responses to inevitable death.

- Discuss real-world examples of death avoidance at personal, cultural, or political levels.

- Invite viewers to reflect on how they personally respond when faced with uncomfortable truths.

Final Thought

Don't Look Up holds a funhouse mirror to humanity's relationship with death. Its message is not subtle, but it is urgent: When we refuse to look at mortality directly, we lose the chance to respond with wisdom, compassion, or courage. The comet may be fictional, but the denial is very real.

Hachi: A Dog's Tale *(2009, G, 1 h 33 min)*

Starring: Richard Gere, Joan Allen

Directed by: Lasse Hallström

Film Description

Based on a true story, this gentle and heartbreaking film follows an Akita puppy who is adopted by a college professor who commutes daily by train. A strong bond forms as Hachi walks his human companion to the station each morning and returns in the afternoon to greet him. When the professor dies suddenly while teaching, Hachi continues his ritual, faithfully waiting at the train station day after day for a man who will never return.

For nine years, Hachi's vigil becomes a quiet act of devotion witnessed by the surrounding community. His presence turns a public space into a living memorial, and his steadfast routine becomes a reminder of love that does not end when death intervenes.

Mortality Themes

- Sudden death and unfinished goodbyes
- Continuing bonds after death
- Loyalty, devotion, and love beyond loss

- Public mourning and memorialization

- How grief can be expressed without words

Discussion Prompts

1. Why does Hachi's grief resonate so strongly even without dialogue?

2. How does routine become a form of remembrance after death?

3. What does the film suggest about love that continues beyond physical presence?

4. How do bystanders and community members respond to prolonged grief?

5. In what ways do humans and animals grieve similarly and differently?

6. What does Hachi's story suggest about the difference between "moving on" and continuing to love after loss?

Movie Pairings and Activities

- Pair the movie with *Marley & Me* (2008) to explore pet loss and unconditional love.

- Or pair it with *A Dog's Purpose* (2017) for animal-centered reflections on meaning and legacy.

- Discuss personal rituals that help keep loved ones present after death.

- Explore how public memorials form organically after loss.

Final Thought

Hachi: A Dog's Tale reminds us that grief does not require language to be profound. Sometimes love shows up every day, at the same place, at the same time, simply refusing to forget. If this movie doesn't wreck you a little, check your pulse.

Little Miss Sunshine *(2006, R, 1 h 41 min)*

Starring: Greg Kinnear, Toni Collette, Steve Carell, Alan Arkin, Paul Dano, Abigail Breslin

Directed by: Jonathan Dayton and Valerie Faris

Film Description

This offbeat family road-trip comedy follows the Hoover family as they pile into a yellow VW bus to support young Olive in her dream of competing in a preteen beauty pageant. Along the way, each family member confronts personal disappointment, fractured dreams, and the tension between winning and simply showing up.

Mortality enters the story quietly but decisively. Grandpa, Olive's biggest cheerleader, dies suddenly during the journey, forcing the family to improvise in ways that are alternately absurd and deeply touching. At the same time, Olive's uncle Frank is recovering from a suicide attempt, bringing questions of despair, purpose, and belonging into the cramped vehicle. The film balances humor and heartbreak with surprising grace.

Mortality Themes

- Sudden death and disrupted plans
- Suicide ideation and recovery
- Family systems under stress
- Failure, acceptance, and redefining success
- Love and solidarity in the face of loss

Discussion Prompts

1. How does the film use humor to make difficult topics more approachable?

2. What does Grandpa's death reveal about the family's values and resilience?

3. How does Frank's storyline broaden the film's exploration of mortality?

4. What does the movie suggest about success versus meaning in life?

5. How does shared adversity reshape the family dynamic?

6. How does the family's willingness to break rules after Grandpa's death reflect their deeper values about dignity and love?

Movie Pairings and Activities

- Pair the movie with *The Big Chill* (1983) to explore loss as a catalyst for self-reflection.

- Or pair it with *Captain Fantastic* (2016) for unconventional families navigating death and values.

- Discuss how humor functions as a coping strategy during crisis.

- Reflect on moments when failure led to unexpected growth.

Final Thought

Little Miss Sunshine reminds us that life rarely unfolds according to plan and that, even in moments marked by death, disappointment, and despair, connection can still steal the spotlight. Sometimes the bravest act is not winning but showing up to dance.

Love and Death *(1975, PG, 1 h 25 min)*

Starring: Woody Allen, Diane Keaton

Directed by: Woody Allen

Film Description

Set in Imperial Russia, this rapid-fire comedy follows Boris Grushenko, a neurotic intellectual, who is terrified of death, skeptical of religion, and obsessed with the meaninglessness of existence. While trying to avoid military service during the Napoleonic Wars, Boris is swept into a series of absurd situations involving philosophy, romance, political intrigue, and ultimately, assassination plots.

Boris' relationship with his cousin Sonja, who is earnest, idealistic, and far more decisive than he is, drives much of the plot. As war, execution, and existential dread loom, Boris spends far more time analyzing death than living life. The film gleefully parodies Russian literature, Tolstoy and Dostoevsky themes, European art films, and existential philosophy, all while asking very real questions about fear, faith, morality, and mortality.

Mortality Themes

- Fear of death and existential anxiety
- The search for meaning in a chaotic world
- War and arbitrary mortality
- Philosophy versus lived experience
- Love as a distraction from or response to death

Discussion Prompts

1. How does Boris' obsession with death shape his choices and relationships?
2. Does the film suggest that philosophy helps or hinders our ability to live fully?
3. How does humor make existential dread more accessible or tolerable?
4. In what ways does Sonja approach life and death differently from Boris?
5. What does the film imply about courage, faith, and action in the face of mortality?
6. What does the film suggest about the cost of thinking about death without actually engaging with life?

Movie Pairings and Activities

- Pair the movie with *The Seventh Seal* (1957) to compare serious versus satirical treatments of death.
- Or pair it with *Hannah and Her Sisters* (1986) for Woody Allen's evolving take on mortality.
- Identify moments where overthinking prevents meaningful action.
- Discuss whether humor is a defense mechanism or a form of wisdom.

Final Thought

Love and Death skewers humanity's tendency to intellectualize mortality instead of engaging with life itself. Beneath the jokes and parodies lies a familiar truth: Worrying endlessly about death can keep us from fully participating in the time we have.

The Man Who Shot Liberty Valance
(1962, Approved, 2 h 3 min)

Starring: James Stewart, John Wayne, Vera Miles, Lee Marvin

Directed by: John Ford

Film Description

This classic Western opens with an apparent contradiction: Senator Ransom Stoddard returns to a dusty frontier town for the funeral of a man few remember. Through a series of flashbacks, the story revisits the violent death of outlaw Liberty Valance and the events that helped transform the lawless Old West into a society governed by laws, institutions, and myths.

As Stoddard recounts his rise from an idealistic lawyer to a national political figure, the film carefully peels back the layers between truth and legend. The death of Liberty Valance becomes a turning point not only for individuals but for an entire culture transitioning from frontier justice to civilization. The question at the heart of the story is not simply who pulled the trigger but what society chooses to remember and why.

Mortality Themes

- Death as a catalyst for cultural and social change
- The passing of an era and collective mourning
- Truth versus myth in how we remember the dead
- Legacy, reputation, and historical memory
- Moral responsibility and unintended consequences

Discussion Prompts

1. Why does the film open with a funeral, and how does that frame the story?

2. What is gained and lost when societies choose legend over truth?

3. How does death function as a turning point for both individuals and institutions?

4. In what ways does the film portray grief for an era rather than a person?

5. How does legacy shape identity long after death?

6. How do funerals function as moments of truth-telling, or truth-editing, in this story?

Movie Pairings and Activities

- Pair the film with *The Grand Budapest Hotel* (2014) to compare how stories shape a legacy.

- Or pair it with *Big Fish* (2003) for contrasting approaches to truth and storytelling.

- Discuss family or cultural stories where legend has overtaken fact.

- Explore how public figures are remembered differently than private individuals.

Final Thought

The Man Who Shot Liberty Valance reminds us that death often marks the end of more than a life. It can signal the closing of an era, the birth of a myth, and the stories we tell to make sense of change. The powerful line, "When the legend becomes truth, print the legend," is instructive. In choosing which truths we preserve, we also decide what kind of world we inherit.

Marley & Me *(2008, PG, 1 h 55 min)*

Starring: Owen Wilson, Jennifer Aniston

Directed by: David Frankel

Film Description

This deceptively simple family film follows newlyweds John and Jenny Grogan as they adopt a rambunctious yellow Labrador puppy named Marley. What begins as a lighthearted comedy about an untrainable dog slowly becomes a life-spanning story that tracks marriage, careers, parenthood, relocation, and the passage of time. Marley is present through it all, marking the family's seasons as he grows from chaos-filled puppyhood into old age.

As Marley's health declines, the film gently but unflinchingly portrays the realities of aging, illness, and saying goodbye to a beloved companion. Without melodrama, it captures the deep emotional bond between humans and animals and the quiet heartbreak that comes when a life intertwined with ours reaches its natural end.

Mortality Themes

- The lifespan gap between humans and pets
- Anticipatory grief and caregiving for aging companions
- Love, attachment, and inevitable loss
- Grief that is socially minimized but deeply felt
- Memory and meaning in ordinary lives

Discussion Prompts

1. Why does pet loss often feel as intense, or more so, as losing a human family member?

2. How does the film prepare the audience for Marley's death without explicitly naming it early on?

3. What rituals or markers of meaning does the family use to honor Marley's life?

4. How does caring for an aging pet mirror caregiving for people later in life?

5. Why do stories about animals often give us permission to express grief more openly?

6. How might acknowledging pet grief more openly change how society understands loss and mourning?

Movie Pairings and Activities

- Pair the movie with *Hachi: A Dog's Tale* (2009) for contrasting depictions of loyalty and loss.

- Or pair it with *Gates of Heaven* (1978) to explore how people memorialize pets.

- Invite viewers to share stories or photos of animals they have loved and lost.

- Discuss how pet loss can be acknowledged in families, workplaces, and communities.

Final Thought

Marley & Me reminds us that love is rarely tidy and that grief is the price of connection. The film gently affirms that a life does not have to be long to be meaningful. Sometimes, the deepest lessons about living and dying arrive on four legs, leave muddy paw prints on our hearts, and stay with us long after the bowl is empty.

Patch Adams *(1998, PG-13, 1 h 55 min)*

Starring: Robin Williams, Monica Potter, Philip Seymour Hoffman

Directed by: Tom Shadyac

Film Description

Based loosely on the life of Dr. Hunter "Patch" Adams, this film follows a medical student who challenges the rigid, impersonal culture of medical training by insisting that laughter, empathy, and genuine human connection are essential parts of healing. Patch treats patients as people first, not diagnoses, often clashing with institutional expectations and professional boundaries.

While much of the film is buoyant and comedic, it takes a darker turn when Patch experiences a devastating personal loss. That moment forces him to confront the limits of optimism, the reality of grief, and the painful truth that compassion does not guarantee protection from heartbreak. The film ultimately wrestles with how caregivers cope when healing is not possible and when love cannot prevent death.

Mortality Themes

- Compassionate care versus clinical detachment
- Grief experienced by caregivers and healers
- The limits of medicine and good intentions
- Meaning-making after loss
- Human connection as comfort when cure is impossible

Discussion Prompts

1. How does Patch Adams redefine what it means to "care" for someone who is suffering?
2. Where does the film draw the line between showing appropriate empathy and crossing a boundary?
3. How does Patch's personal loss change his philosophy, if at all?
4. What does the film suggest about how medical professionals are trained to handle death?
5. Can humor be both healing and inadequate at the same time?
6. How can caregivers honor their own grief without losing their capacity to care for others?

Movie Pairings and Activities

- Pair the movie with *Wit* (2001) to contrast emotional engagement with clinical detachment.
- Or pair it with *The Doctor* (1991) to explore transformation through illness and loss.

- Discuss what makes someone feel truly "seen" during illness or grief.

- Invite healthcare professionals to reflect on moments when connection mattered more than cure.

Final Thought

Patch Adams reminds us that medicine may extend life but compassion gives it texture and meaning. When healing fails, presence still matters. Laughter may not save us from loss, but kindness can carry us through it, and sometimes that is the most human medicine of all.

Philadelphia *(1993, PG-13, 2 h 5 min)*

Starring: Tom Hanks, Denzel Washington, Jason Robards, Mary Steenburgen

Directed by: Jonathan Demme

Film Description

This landmark drama tells the story of Andrew Beckett, a talented young attorney, who is fired from his prestigious Philadelphia law firm after his employers discover he has AIDS. Convinced his dismissal is rooted in discrimination, Andrew hires Joe Miller, a personal injury lawyer who initially carries his own fear and prejudice about AIDS and homosexuality.

As the lawsuit unfolds, the film follows Andrew's physical decline alongside the emotional and moral growth of those around him. We witness the quiet realities of dying during the AIDS crisis, from hospital rooms and home care to moments of tenderness, anger, dignity, and love. The legal battle becomes a backdrop for a deeply human story about justice, compassion, and what it means to be seen as fully human at the end of life.

Mortality Themes

- Terminal illness and physical decline

- Stigma, fear, and social isolation around death

- Chosen family and caregiving

- Dignity in dying

- Moral awakening and empathy
- Legacy through courage and truth-telling

Discussion Prompts

1. How does the film portray the difference between legal justice and human justice?

2. In what ways does Andrew assert dignity and agency as his body weakens?

3. How does Joe Miller change over the course of the film, and what prompts that change?

4. What does the film reveal about how fear shapes society's response to illness and death?

5. How might this story resonate differently today than it did in the early 1990s?

6. How does witnessing Andrew's dying challenge viewers to examine their own fears about illness, stigma, and mortality?

Movie Pairings and Activities

- Pair the film with *Angels in America* (2003 TV mini-series) for a broader view of the AIDS crisis and spiritual reckoning.
- Or pair it with *The Normal Heart* (2014) to deepen discussion on activism, anger, and loss.
- Discuss the role of advocacy at the end of life, both legal and personal.
- Invite reflection on how stigma can compound suffering for the dying and their families.

Final Thought

Philadelphia asks us to confront not just how people die but how they are treated while dying. It reminds us that compassion is learned, dignity must be defended, and love often shows up in the quietest rooms. Andrew Beckett's legacy is not only the case he fought but the humanity he insisted on keeping until his final breath.

Sunshine Cleaning *(2008, R, 1 h 31 min)*

Starring: Amy Adams, Emily Blunt, Alan Arkin

Directed by: Christine Jeffs

Film Description

In this offbeat comedy drama, sisters Rose and Norah Lorkowski stumble into an unlikely line of work: professional crime scene cleanup. Armed with hazmat suits, industrial cleaners, and very little emotional preparation, they scrub homes after violent deaths, suicides, and unattended passings.

As they clean up blood, brains, and biohazards, the sisters are forced to confront the messier residue in their own lives. Both are still shaped by their mother's suicide years earlier, an event that fractured their family and left grief largely unspoken. Their new business becomes an accidental form of exposure therapy, placing them face-to-face with death while they slowly begin to address their own unresolved pain, failures, and hopes for something better.

Mortality Themes

- Suicide and unresolved grief

- Emotional labor surrounding death

- Death work and society's discomfort with it

- Family systems shaped by loss

- Avoidance versus confrontation of grief

- Meaning-making through service

Discussion Prompts

1. How does working with physical death force the sisters to confront emotional death in their own lives?

2. What does the film suggest about society's need for death work and its reluctance to acknowledge it?

3. How does unresolved grief show up differently in Rose and Norah?

4. In what ways does cleaning become both a metaphor for healing and an imperfect solution?

5. How does humor function as a coping mechanism in the face of trauma and loss?

6. How does proximity to death change what the sisters believe for their own futures?

Movie Pairings and Activities

- Pair the film with *Departures* (2008) to compare different forms of death work and emotional engagement.

- Or pair it with *Six Feet Under* (2001-2005, TV series) for a deeper exploration of families shaped by death-related professions.

- Discuss invisible labor around death and who is tasked with it.

- Invite reflection on what emotional "cleanup" people avoid in their own lives.

Final Thought

Sunshine Cleaning reminds us that, while blood and biohazards can be scrubbed away, grief clings differently. It settles into families, habits, and unspoken memories. Healing does not come from erasing the mess but from finally standing in it, acknowledging what was lost, and choosing to move forward anyway.

Weekend at Bernie's *(1989, PG-13, 1 h 37 min)*

Starring: Andrew McCarthy, Jonathan Silverman, Terry Kiser

Directed by: Ted Kotcheff

Film Description

In this sun-drenched slapstick comedy, young insurance company employees Larry and Richard arrive at their boss Bernie Lomax's beach house for what they think will be a lavish weekend. Instead, they discover Bernie is very much dead. Rather than reporting the death or fleeing the scene, panic and self-preservation take over. They prop up Bernie's corpse and spend the weekend pretending he is still alive.

What follows is an escalating parade of absurd situations as Bernie is dragged through parties, boat rides, encounters with criminals, and romantic misunderstandings, all while no one seems to notice he is deceased. The film leans hard into physical comedy and farce, but beneath the silliness is an uncomfortable truth about how easily death can be ignored when it is inconvenient, inconvenient to power, money, or social comfort.

Mortality Themes

- Denial and avoidance of death

- Treating death as an inconvenience

- Fear-driven decision-making around mortality

- Social performance versus reality

- Dehumanization of the dead

Discussion Prompts

1. Why do Larry and Richard choose denial over responsibility when faced with Bernie's death?

2. How does the film exaggerate society's tendency to ignore death when it disrupts comfort or status?

3. What makes this treatment of a corpse feel humorous, disturbing, or both?

4. How does Bernie's continued "presence" comment on power and identity after death?

5. What does the film suggest about accountability when death enters the picture?

6. What does the film reveal about how quickly death can strip someone of dignity when no on is willing to acknowledge it?

Movie Pairings and Activities

- Pair the film with *The Death of Stalin* (2017) for a darker satire about power struggles after death.

- Or pair it with *Don't Look Up* (2021) to compare denial at personal versus societal levels.

- Discuss cultural discomfort with death and how humor is often used to deflect fear.

- Explore how denial shows up in real-world responses to illness, dying, or loss.

Final Thought

Weekend at Bernie's may look like pure nonsense on the surface, but its enduring appeal lies in how perfectly it captures human denial. When death threatens comfort, reputation, or control, pretending everything is fine can feel easier than facing reality. The joke works because it is extreme, but the impulse behind it is deeply familiar.

Hard-to-Categorize Mortality Movies: Closing Thoughts

If these films teach us anything, it is that mortality does not need a spotlight to matter. It can hover in the background, sneak in through humor, or arrive disguised as inconvenience, irony, or absurdity. Even when death is not the main event, it still shapes behavior, exposes values, and asks questions we cannot ignore for long.

The beauty of this category lies in its unpredictability. These movies remind us that life does not unfold in tidy genres, and neither does grief, meaning, or transformation. Sometimes the most instructive moments about death appear when we least expect them, right in the middle of a comedy, a road trip, or a chocolate shop in winter.

If you find yourself laughing, unsettled, or suddenly reflective after watching one of these films, that is the point. Mortality does not always announce itself. Sometimes it just taps you on the shoulder and waits for you to notice.

DOCUMENTARIES

Introduction

Documentaries invite us to sit closer to death than fiction ever could. These films do not rely on actors, scripts, or imagined outcomes. Instead, they bear witness to real people navigating illness, dying, caregiving, ritual, and remembrance. There is no tidy arc, no guarantee of catharsis, and no promise of resolution. What they offer instead is truth, presence, and perspective.

The documentaries in this chapter pull back the curtain on how death actually unfolds in hospitals, homes, hospices, cemeteries, and forests. They show us the beauty and the mess, the courage and the fear, the wisdom that can emerge when people are allowed to face mortality honestly. Some films challenge medical culture. Others illuminate alternative ways of caring for the dead or honoring the dying. All of them ask us to slow down and really look.

Watching these films is an act of learning and of humility. They remind us that death is not an abstraction; it is personal, relational, and deeply shaped by the choices we make long before the final days arrive.

Being Mortal: Frontline Documentary *(2017, 54 min)*

Starring: Dr. Atul Gawande

Directed by: Frontline (PBS)

Film Description

This frontline documentary follows Dr. Atul Gawande, a Boston surgeon and author of the influential book *Being Mortal*, as he examines how modern medicine handles aging, chronic illness, and dying. Through patient stories, clinical encounters, and his own self-reflection, Gawande reveals how often doctors are trained to fight disease but not prepared to talk honestly about decline, limits, or death.

The film exposes a medical culture that prioritizes intervention over conversation even when aggressive treatment may increase suffering rather than improve the quality of life. By highlighting moments where listening matters more than fixing, *Being Mortal* reframes end-of-life care as a deeply human process rather than a medical failure.

Mortality Themes

- Death as a natural part of life, not a medical defeat
- The importance of honest conversations about goals and values
- Quality of life versus life-prolonging treatment
- Aging, autonomy, and dignity
- The emotional burden carried by patients, families, and clinicians

Discussion Prompts

1. Why are conversations about death so difficult for many doctors and patients?

2. How does the medical system sometimes confuse "doing everything" with "doing what matters"?

3. What does a good death look like, and who gets to define it?

4. How might earlier conversations about values change medical decisions at the end of life?

5. What role should families play when a loved one can no longer speak for themselves?

6. How might normalizing conversations about death earlier in life change how people experience aging and illness?

Movie Pairings and Activities

- Pair the film with *Wit* (2001) or *The Doctor* (1991) to explore patient experience from the inside.

- Write or review an advance directive or values statement.

- Invite participants to practice asking the "What matters to you?" question rather than "What's the matter?"

Final Thought

Being Mortal reminds us that medicine is at its best when it serves the person, not just the diagnosis. By showing what happens when we talk honestly about dying, the film offers a powerful invitation to reclaim death as part of life and to make space for care that honors meaning, comfort, and choice.

Gates of Heaven *(1978, 1 h 25 min)*

Directed by: Errol Morris

Film Description

This quietly eccentric documentary explores a pet cemetery in California and the people who choose to bury their animals there. Through a series of unpolished deeply sincere interviews, owners speak at length about their deceased pets, the love they shared, and the care taken to memorialize them properly.

What begins as a film about animals gradually reveals itself as a study of human grief. Without narration or commentary, the camera simply listens as people articulate loss, devotion, regret, and meaning. By focusing on pets rather than people, the film sidesteps many social taboos around mourning and allows grief to appear in its most honest, unguarded form.

Mortality Themes

- Grief and attachment

- The legitimacy of pet loss

- Memorialization and ritual

- Love as a measure of loss

- How ordinary people make meaning after death

Discussion Prompts

1. Why is grief over pets sometimes minimized or dismissed by society?

2. How do the rituals surrounding pet death mirror those used for humans?

3. What does this film suggest about the universality of grief?

4. How does the absence of narration affect the way we engage with loss?

5. In what ways do memorials help the living continue bonds with the dead?

6. How does focusing on pet loss make it easier, or harder, to acknowledge our own mortality?

Movie Pairings and Activities

- Pair the film with *Hachi: A Dog's Tale* (2009) or *Marley & Me* (2008) for a deeper look at pet loss.

- Invite participants to share a story about an animal they loved.

- Discuss which losses society "permits" us to grieve openly.

Final Thought

Gates of Heaven gently reminds us that grief does not measure itself by species. Love is love, and loss is loss. By honoring the depth of feeling people have for their pets, the film quietly makes the case that all grief deserves space, respect, and ritual.

How to Die in Oregon *(2011, 1 h 47 min)*

Directed by: Peter Richardson

Film Description

This documentary follows several terminally ill Oregonians who choose to use the state's Death with Dignity Act, the first medical aid in dying law passed in the United States. Through intimate access to patients and their families, the film shows the physical, emotional, and ethical realities of facing death with a prescribed timeline. It also documents the parallel effort to pass a similar law in Washington state, offering political, medical, and personal perspectives on an issue that remains deeply complex and often misunderstood.

Mortality Themes

- Medical aid in dying
- Patient autonomy and informed consent
- Fear of suffering versus fear of death
- Family dynamics at the end of life
- Ethics, legality, and cultural attitudes toward dying
- Death as a process, not a single moment

Discussion Prompts

1. What motivations did participants express for choosing medical aid in dying, and how did these differ from person to person?

2. How did family members respond to the choice, and what tensions or supports emerged?

3. What role did physicians play, and how did their responsibilities differ from traditional end-of-life care?

4. How does watching real people navigate this process differ from the fictional portrayals of assisted dying?

5. Did the documentary challenge or reinforce your own beliefs about autonomy, dignity, or timing at the end of life?

6. How does witnessing real end-of-life choices complicate simplistic arguments for or against medical aid in dying?

Movie Pairings and Activities

- Pair the film with *Blackbird* (2019) or *Whose Life Is It Anyway?* (1981) for fictional explorations of autonomy and choice.

- Or pair it with *Being Mortal* (2017, Frontline) for a broader view of medical culture and end-of-life conversations.

- Review your state's laws regarding medical aid in dying and discuss how geography shapes end-of-life options.

- Use the film as a springboard to talk about advance directives, value statements, and what matters the most at the end of life.

Final Thought

How to Die in Oregon does not argue for or against medical aid in dying. Instead, it bears witness. By centering real people rather than abstract debates, the film reminds us that end-of-life decisions are rarely ideological. They are personal, relational, and grounded in love, fear, and the desire for relief. Whether viewers agree with the choices shown or not, the documentary invites a deeper, more humane conversation about how we care for one another when time is short.

Last Ecstatic Days *(2024, 1 h 15 min)*

Directed by: Ethan Sisser and collaborators

Featuring: Ethan Sisser

Film Description

This intimate and unflinching documentary follows Ethan Sisser, a young man dying of brain cancer, during the final phase of his life on hospice. Rather than turning away from the realities of dying, the film stays close. We witness physical decline, emotional vulnerability, moments of fear, tenderness, humor, and connection.

The camera does not sensationalize or soften the process. Instead, it bears quiet witness as Ethan navigates the daily realities of terminal illness while supported by hospice care and loved ones. The result is a rare and deeply human portrait of dying as lived experience rather than medical abstraction.

Mortality Themes

- Hospice and end-of-life care
- The physical realities of dying
- Presence and witnessing
- Vulnerability and dignity
- Death as a lived process, not a single moment

Discussion Prompts

1. How does seeing the dying process up close change your understanding of death?

2. What role does hospice play in shaping Ethan's final days?

3. Which moments felt the most difficult to watch, and why?

4. How does this film challenge the cultural avoidance of dying?

5. What does "a good death" mean after watching this documentary?

6. What does it mean to truly "bear witness" to someone's dying, and how does this film invite or challenge that kind of presence?

Movie Pairings and Activities

- Pair the film with *Being Mortal* (2017) or *Solace: Wisdom of the Dying* (2008).

- Invite a hospice professional to discuss what hospice actually provides.

- Journal about what presence might look like at the end of life, both for the dying and the living.

Final Thought

Last Ecstatic Days does not ask us to feel inspired or comforted; it asks us to stay. By allowing death to be seen rather than hidden, the film offers one of the most honest gifts cinema can give: a chance to witness dying with clarity, compassion, and respect.

Solace: Wisdom of the Dying *(2008, 1 h 24 min)*

Directed by: Camille Adair

Film Description

This reflective documentary grew out of director Camille Adair's work as a hospice nurse, shaped by years of sitting at the bedsides of dying patients and supporting their families. Rather than focusing on crisis or medical intervention, *Solace* slows down and listens. Through intimate conversations, it invites viewers into the lived experiences of people facing the end of life, alongside insights from caregivers, clinicians, and spiritual thinkers.

The film gently reframes death not as a medical failure but as a meaningful and natural human process. It emphasizes presence, listening, and the emotional and spiritual dimensions of dying, offering a counterbalance to a culture that often treats death as something to be fought at all costs.

Mortality Themes

- Death as a natural and sacred process
- Hospice philosophy and end-of-life care
- Listening, presence, and compassion
- Meaning-making at the end of life
- Shifting from cure-focused to comfort-focused care

Discussion Prompts

1. How does this film challenge common cultural narratives about death as failure?

2. What moments or voices stayed with you the most strongly, and why?

3. How does hospice care differ from typical medical treatment at the end of life?

4. What does the film suggest about the role of listening when someone is dying?

5. How might our healthcare system change if death were approached as a sacred process?

6. How might adopting a hospice philosophy earlier in illness change both living and dying?

Movie Pairings and Activities

- Pair the film with *Being Mortal* (2017) or *Last Ecstatic Days* (2024).
- Host a facilitated discussion with a hospice nurse or chaplain.
- Write about what would help you feel supported and heard at the end of life.

Final Thought

Solace: Wisdom of the Dying offers no dramatic climax or tidy conclusions. Its power lies in its quiet insistence that dying deserves time, attention, and reverence. By honoring death as part of life rather than its opposite, the film gently teaches that how we die is shaped by how we listen, care, and remain present to one another until the very end.

A Will for the Woods *(2014, TV-G, 1 h 33 min)*

Directed by: Amy Browne

Film Description

This gentle, intimate documentary follows Clark Wang, a young man living with lymphoma, as he prepares for his own death with intention, curiosity, and care. Alongside his partner Jane, Clark visits the North Carolina woodland where he will be buried, learning about green burial practices and imagining his body's return to the natural world. Rather than focusing on decline, the film centers on Clark's passions, relationships, and values as he approaches the end of his life.

The documentary offers a rare look at home funerals and environmentally sustainable burial practices while also capturing the emotional landscape of a couple facing death together. Clark's calm, thoughtful approach invites viewers to consider death planning as an act of love, agency, and environmental stewardship.

Mortality Themes

- Green burial and environmentally conscious death care
- Home funerals and family-led rituals
- Preparing for death with intention
- Love, partnership, and shared decision-making
- Legacy through values rather than possessions

Discussion Prompts

1. How does Clark's approach to death planning differ from common cultural norms?

2. What emotions arose while watching Clark and Jane navigate these conversations together?

3. How does green burial change the way we think about the body after death?

4. What does the film suggest about autonomy and choice at the end of life?

5. How might planning ahead ease the burden on loved ones?

6. How does aligning death care with personal values reshape the idea of legacy?

Movie Pairings and Activities

- Pair the film with *Being Mortal* (2017) or *Solace: Wisdom of the Dying* (2008).

- Research local green burial or home funeral options.

- Write a values-based "will" describing what matters the most to you beyond possessions.

Final Thought

A Will for the Woods reminds us that death planning does not have to be grim or clinical. It can be creative, values driven, and deeply loving. By choosing how his body will return to the earth, Clark shows that, even in dying, we can make choices that reflect who we are, what we cherish, and how we hope to be remembered.

Documentaries: Closing Thoughts

Documentaries strip away the comforting distance of fiction. There are no scripts, no swelling soundtracks to cue our emotions, and no tidy endings. What we are left with are real people, real bodies, real families, and real moments when mortality moves from theory into lived experience. These films invite us not to watch death from afar but to sit beside it.

Together, these documentaries reveal death as a deeply human process rather than a medical failure or moral abstraction. They show how people prepare, resist, accept, question, and sometimes choose the timing of their own endings. From green burials to hospice care, from pet loss to medical aid in dying, these stories illuminate the many ways we seek meaning, agency, and dignity when life is nearing its close.

Perhaps most powerfully, these films remind us that the conversations we avoid are often the ones that matter the most. Watching others navigate illness, caregiving, legacy, and choice can clarify our own values and spark discussions we might otherwise postpone. If these documentaries encourage you to talk more openly with loved ones, to document your wishes, or simply to listen more carefully to those who are dying, then they have done important work.

In bearing witness to real lives and real deaths, these films do not tell us how to die; they ask us how we want to live, right up to the end.

TELEVISION SHOWS AND SERIES

Introduction

Television has a unique relationship with mortality. Unlike films, which ask us to sit with death for a single contained experience, TV shows invite us to live alongside characters over time. We watch them age, struggle, love, lose, and sometimes die, often after years of shared history. When death appears in a television series, it can feel startlingly personal, like losing someone we know.

Because television enters our homes regularly and often casually, it has a quiet power to introduce conversations about death, dying, grief, and legacy without requiring a formal "movie night." A thirty-minute sitcom episode can tackle funeral planning with humor. A miniseries can walk us through terminal illness with intimacy and nuance. Long-running dramas can normalize conversations about mortality simply by returning to them again and again.

The shows in this chapter span decades, genres, and tones, from laugh-out-loud comedies to unflinching dramas. Some episodes approach death sideways, through satire or surprise. Others meet it head-on, offering raw depictions of illness, loss, medical decision-making, and the messy aftermath left behind. Together, they show how mortality is not an interruption to life's story but a central thread woven throughout it.

All in the Family: "Stretch Cunningham, Goodbye"
(1977, Season 7, Episode 19, 30 min)

Starring: Carroll O'Connor, Jean Stapleton, Rob Reiner, Sally Struthers

Created by: Norman Lear

Film Description

In this classic episode, Archie Bunker is tasked with delivering a eulogy for a coworker he barely knew: Stretch Cunningham. Confident in his assumptions and armed with half-remembered anecdotes, Archie prepares a speech that reflects more about his own worldview than the man being honored. When he arrives at the funeral, he is confronted with a revelation that upends everything he thought he knew about Stretch. What follows is a rare moment of humility for Archie and a surprisingly tender exploration of how little we sometimes know about the people we share our lives with.

Mortality Themes

- Funerals as moments of reckoning and revelation
- The complexity and hidden dimensions of personal identity
- The risks of assumptions when honoring the dead
- Eulogy writing as both tribute and responsibility

Discussion Prompts

1. What does Archie's initial eulogy reveal about him rather than Stretch?

2. How did the surprise at the funeral change Archie's understanding of his coworker?

3. What responsibilities do we carry when speaking for someone who can no longer speak for themselves?

4. How might this episode change the way viewers think about writing a eulogy?

5. Why do funerals sometimes reveal truths that everyday life allows people to hide?

6.   How might this episode encourage viewers to be more curious about the inner lives of people they think they already know?

Movie Pairings and Activities

- Pair the episode with *The Mary Tyler Moore Show: "Chuckles Bites the Dust"* (1975) for a look at humor and decorum at funerals.

- Invite participants to write a short eulogy for someone they know well, then reflect on what might still be missing.

- Use the episode as a conversation starter about how funerals can challenge stereotypes and assumptions.

Final Thought

With its trademark blend of humor and discomfort, *All in the Family* reminds us that death often reveals truths we overlooked in life. This episode gently nudges viewers to approach remembrance with curiosity, humility, and a willingness to be surprised.

Angels in America *(2003, HBO Miniseries, TV-MA, 6 h)*

Starring: Al Pacino, Meryl Streep, Emma Thompson, Justin Kirk, Patrick Wilson, Mary-Louise Parker

Directed by: Mike Nichols

Film Description

Set in mid-1980s America at the height of the AIDS crisis, *Angels in America* weaves together the lives of several characters whose paths intersect through illness, politics, love, and spiritual reckoning. As bodies fail and relationships strain, angels appear, visions erupt, and reality bends. The miniseries moves between hospital rooms, courtrooms, bedrooms, and celestial visitations, capturing both the intimacy of dying and the sweeping social consequences of a nation in denial. It is at once deeply personal and unapologetically political, confronting mortality alongside power, fear, and faith.

Mortality Themes

- Illness as a confrontation with mortality and meaning
- Denial versus acceptance in the face of death
- Legacy, justice, and moral accountability
- Spirituality, transcendence, and the search for purpose
- Resilience and connection amid widespread loss

Discussion Prompts

1. How does the series portray different responses to terminal illness and impending death?

2. In what ways do denial and fear shape the characters' choices, both personally and politically?

3. How does *Angels in America* link individual mortality with social responsibility and justice?

4. What role do spirituality and supernatural elements play in making sense of suffering and loss?

5. How does the series portray caregiving as both an act of love and a source of exhaustion or conflict?

6. What does the series suggest about remembering the dead when society would rather forget them?

Movie Pairings and Activities

- Pair the series with *Philadelphia* (1993) for a grounded courtroom-centered portrayal of AIDS-era mortality.
- Or pair it with *Wit* (2001) to contrast spiritual transcendence with clinical realism.
- Invite discussion on how public health crises shape cultural attitudes toward death.
- Use excerpts to explore how storytelling preserves dignity in the face of stigma.

Final Thought

Angels in America refuses to look away from death, suffering, or injustice. Instead, it insists that bearing witness is an act of love and resistance. In giving voice to the dying and demanding accountability from the living, the series reminds us that mortality is never just personal. It is political, spiritual, and deeply human.

Dying for Sex *(2025, Hulu-Disney+ Miniseries, TV-MA, 4 h, Eight 30-min Episodes)*

Starring: Michelle Williams, Jenny Slate, Rob Delaney

Directed by: Shannon Murphy

Film Description

Inspired by the real-life story and podcast of Molly Kochan, *Dying for Sex* follows a woman who receives a diagnosis of metastatic breast cancer and decides not to spend her remaining time trying to preserve a marriage that no longer fits. Instead, with the unwavering support of her best friend Nikki, Molly sets out to explore her sexuality, desires, and sense of agency before she dies. The series balances frank discussions of illness, treatment, and bodily decline with humor, vulnerability, and moments of surprising joy. It is explicit, emotionally honest, and unapologetically centered on autonomy and pleasure at the end of life.

Mortality Themes

- Terminal illness and bodily autonomy
- Sexuality, identity, and desire near the end of life
- Friendship as primary caregiving and emotional support
- Reclaiming agency in the face of medicalized dying
- Living fully rather than quietly fading away

Discussion Prompts

1. How does the series challenge cultural assumptions about sexuality and illness?

2. In what ways does Molly's diagnosis free her rather than limit her?

3. How is friendship portrayed as a form of end-of-life care alongside or instead of family?

4. What does the show suggest about quality of life versus societal expectations of "good" dying?

5. How does the series redefine what it means to live well when time is clearly limited?

6. What discomforts might viewers experience watching this series, and what do those reactions reveal about cultural attitudes toward death and sex?

Movie Pairings and Activities

- Pair the episodes with *50/50* (2011) to compare humor as a coping mechanism during serious illness.

- Or pair them with *Wit* (2001) to contrast emotional vulnerability with institutional medical care.

- Use the episode as a springboard for conversations about intimacy, consent, and autonomy in serious illness.

- Discuss how end-of-life narratives change when pleasure and desire are centered.

Final Thought

Dying for Sex insists that dying does not cancel desire, curiosity, or the need to feel fully alive. By refusing to sanitize or sentimentalize the end of life, the series offers a bold reminder that autonomy includes the right to pleasure, honesty, and self-definition, even, and especially, at the very end. It may make you laugh, blush, cry, and rethink everything you thought you knew about how we're "supposed" to die. And that, frankly, is its greatest gift.

Grace and Frankie: "The Party"
(2016, Netflix Series, Season 2, Episode 12, TV-MA, 30 min)

Starring: Lily Tomlin, Jane Fonda, June Diane Raphael, Brooklyn Decker

Directed by: Marta Kauffman and Howard J. Morris (series creators, episode directed by Rebecca Asher)

Film Description

In this episode of the comedy-drama series *Grace and Frankie*, Frankie's close friend Babe reveals that she has a terminal illness and plans to use medical aid in dying. Rather than letting the end of Babe's life be quiet or grim, Frankie helps her throw an exuberant farewell party that celebrates friendship, joy, honesty, and the life Babe has lived. The episode balances humor and tenderness, offering a rare television portrayal of chosen death framed through agency, love, and community rather than fear.

Mortality Themes

- Medical aid in dying and end-of-life autonomy
- Friendship as spiritual and emotional support at death
- Celebratory rituals before death
- Choosing joy and meaning in the face of mortality
- Honoring final wishes while the person is still alive

Discussion Prompts

1. How does this episode challenge the common portrayals of dying on television?
2. What role does celebration play in helping people face death?
3. How do Frankie and Babe model supportive end-of-life companionship?
4. What emotions did humor allow space for that a solemn tone might not?
5. How does agency over one's death affect the grief of those left behind?
6. How might openly discussing death *before* it happens change how we grieve afterward?

Movie Pairings and Activities

- Pair the episode with *How to Die in Oregon* (2011) for a documentary perspective on medical aid in dying.

- Or pair it with *The Farewell* (2019) to compare anticipatory grief across cultures.

- Invite viewers to design their own "living goodbye" gathering, real or imagined.

- Hold a group discussion on what makes a meaningful ending to a life well lived.

Final Thought

This episode reminds us that death does not cancel joy, humor, or connection. Sometimes the most loving thing we can do is show up fully, raise a glass, and say goodbye while the person we love can still hear us laugh.

The Kominsky Method: "An Agent Grieves"
(2018, Netflix Series, Season 1, Episode 2, TV-MA, 30 min)

Starring: Michael Douglas, Alan Arkin, Sarah Baker

Directed by: Chuck Lorre (series creator, episode directed by Andy Tennant)

Film Description

This episode from the award-winning Netflix comedy drama *The Kominsky Method* centers on Sandy Kominsky, an aging acting coach navigating illness, loss, and the realities of getting older in Hollywood. After Eileen, the wife of Sandy's longtime agent and close friend Norman, dies, the episode pivots to the fallout of that death, including funeral planning and the emotional chaos that follows. Eileen's carefully prepared letter of instruction guides the family through an extravagant highly personalized funeral. The result is a cathartic mix of chaos, humor, love, and the very practical realities of death planning. The entire series provides an instructive look at how we contend with illness, death, grief, and estate issues.

Mortality Themes

- Funeral and estate planning as an act of care for survivors
- Letters of instruction and advance planning
- Friendship, grief, and aging
- Sudden death and its logistical aftermath
- Humor as a coping mechanism in loss

Discussion Prompts

1. How does the letter of instruction change the funeral experience for Norman?
2. What does this episode suggest about the emotional value of planning ahead?
3. How does humor function as both relief and avoidance in the face of death?
4. What moments reveal the difference between legal documents and personal guidance?
5. How does aging reshape friendships and perspectives on mortality?
6. How might writing a letter of instruction change the way someone thinks about their own death while they are still alive?

Movie Pairings and Activities

- Pair the episode with *The Loved One* (1965) for a satirical look at funeral excess.
- Or pair it with *The Last Word* (2017) to explore legacy and self-authorship.
- Invite viewers to draft a simple letter of instruction outlining their personal wishes.
- Discuss in a group what makes a funeral feel authentic versus performative.

Final Thought

This episode makes a compelling case that planning ahead is not about control but about kindness. When we leave clear guidance behind, we spare the people we love from guessing, arguing, and wondering if they got it right.

The Mary Tyler Moore Show: "Chuckles Bites the Dust"
(1975, Season 6, Episode 7, 30 min)

Starring: Mary Tyler Moore, Ed Asner, Valerie Harper, Ted Knight, Gavin MacLeod

Directed by: Jay Sandrich

Film Description

When beloved children's entertainer Chuckles the Clown dies in a bizarre parade accident, the staff at WJM-TV struggles to respond appropriately. Mary Richards insists that death is a serious matter and is deeply uncomfortable with her coworkers' irreverent humor. However, at Chuckles' funeral, the tension between propriety and authenticity reaches a breaking point. What follows is a masterclass in comic timing and emotional truth, revealing how people cope with death in wildly different ways.

The closing scene where Mary and her colleagues discuss each one's individual preferences for their funerals and disposition methods provides a perfect introduction to preplanning conversations.

Mortality Themes

- Humor and laughter as responses to death
- Social expectations around "appropriate" grief
- Funerals as emotional pressure cookers
- The clash between public decorum and private feeling
- Grief expressed through irony, discomfort, and release

Discussion Prompts

1. Why does Mary struggle so much with her coworkers' humor about Chuckles' death?

2. What does this episode suggest about the many valid ways people grieve?

3. How do funerals amplify emotions that have been carefully contained?

4. When does humor cross a line, and who gets to decide where that line is?

5. How might this episode open conversations about personalization in funerals?

6. How does this episode help normalize emotional messiness in moments when people expect composure?

Movie Pairings and Activities

- Pair the episode with *Steel Magnolias* (1989) for humor layered over profound loss.

- Or pair it with *The Loved One* (1965) to examine satire in death rituals.

- Discuss what kind of tone feels right at a funeral and why that varies.

- Share stories of moments when laughter unexpectedly surfaced during grief.

Final Thought

"Chuckles Bites the Dust" endures because it tells a deep truth with impeccable timing: Grief does not follow rules, and laughter is not the opposite of sorrow. Sometimes, it is the only way through.

Mike and Molly: "Joyce's Will Be Done"
(2016, Season 6, Episode 5, 19 min)

Starring: Swoosie Kurtz, Melissa McCarthy, Billy Gardell, Katy Mixon

Directed by: Bob Koherr

Film Description

After their yoga instructor collapses and dies mid-class, Molly's larger-than-life mother Joyce is jolted into confronting her own mortality. She decides it is time to get her affairs in order, including drafting a will and making plans for what happens after she is gone. What begins as a practical exercise quickly spirals into family conflict, bruised feelings, and comedic chaos as Molly and her sister react to Joyce's choices. The episode uses humor to expose how uncomfortable, emotional, and revealing estate planning conversations can be.

Mortality Themes

- Sudden death as a wake-up call

- Advance medical directives and wills

- Family dynamics and unresolved resentments

- Control versus care at the end of life

- Inheritance as both practical and deeply emotional

Discussion Prompts

1. What specifically triggers Joyce to take action about her estate, and why does it feel urgent?

2. How do Molly and her sister respond differently to their mother's planning?

3. What fears about aging, control, and being forgotten surface during the episode?

4. Why do conversations about money and possessions often carry more emotional weight than expected?

5. How might humor make estate planning discussions more approachable or more volatile?

6. How might earlier, calmer conversations about death change the emotional tone of this episode?

Movie Pairings and Activities

- Pair the episode with *The Six Wives of Henry Lefay* (2009) for inheritance-driven chaos.

- Or pair it with *About Schmidt* (2002) to contrast comic and dramatic approaches to legacy.

- Invite viewers to list what they would want included in a letter of instruction.

- Discuss how planning ahead can reduce conflict rather than create it.

Final Thought

"Joyce's Will Be Done" proves that estate planning is never just about paperwork; it is about identity, fairness, love, and the very human fear of losing control. Laughter may not make these conversations easy, but it can make them possible.

Six Feet Under *(2001-2005, HBO Series, TV-MA, 5 Seasons)*

Starring: Peter Krause, Michael C. Hall, Frances Conroy, Lauren Ambrose, Rachel Griffiths

Directed by: Created by Alan Ball

Film Description

This Emmy Award-winning HBO series centers on the Fisher family who run an independent funeral home in Los Angeles. Every episode opens with a death, sometimes shocking, sometimes mundane, followed by the funeral arrangements and the ripple effects that the loss creates for both the bereaved families and the Fishers themselves.

Alongside embalming rooms and visitation chapels, the series explores the private lives, relationships, and inner struggles of the Fisher family. One of its signature storytelling devices is the appearance of the dead speaking to the living, not as ghosts but as manifestations of memory, guilt, love, and unfinished business.

The show was produced with consultation from funeral directors and is notable for its realistic portrayal of funeral industry practices and emerging trends. At the same time, it is deeply philosophical, using death as a lens through which to examine sex, identity, faith, addiction, family loyalty, and the search for meaning. As an HBO series, it includes explicit language and sexual content that may limit its suitability for public or classroom settings.

Mortality Themes

- Death as an everyday, unavoidable presence
- Funeral practices and industry realities
- Family dynamics under the constant pressure of loss
- Continuing bonds with the dead
- Identity, legacy, and impermanence
- Ethical and environmental shifts in death care

Discussion Prompts

1. How does beginning every episode with a death shape the viewer's relationship to mortality?

2. What role do the imagined conversations with the dead play in the characters' grief and decision-making?

3. How does the series portray the tension between professionalism and personal emotion in death-care work?

4. In what ways does repeated exposure to death change the Fisher family over time?

5. How does the show challenge or reinforce cultural expectations around funerals and mourning?

6. How does the series influence viewers' comfort level with discussing death openly in their own lives?

Movie Pairings and Activities

- Pair the series with *Departures* (2008) to compare Western and non-Western funeral traditions.

- Or pair it with *Sunshine Cleaning* (2008) for another behind-the-scenes look at death work.

- Watch a single episode and map the emotional journey of the bereaved family.

- Discuss how fantasy conversations with the dead mirror real inner dialogue during grief.

Final Thought

Six Feet Under does not ask whether death will come; it asks how we live while it does. By placing mortality at the center of everyday life, the series reminds us that death is not the opposite of living but the frame that gives it shape, urgency, and meaning.

The Twilight Zone
(1959–1964, CBS Television Series, TV-PG, 5 Seasons)

Starring: Rod Serling, with rotating casts including Burgess Meredith, Agnes Moorehead, William Shatner, Jack Klugman, Robert Redford

Directed by: Various; created, written, and narrated by Rod Serling

Film Description

This landmark anthology series created by Rod Serling uses science fiction, fantasy, and psychological drama to explore the human condition under extraordinary circumstances. Each self-contained episode drops ordinary people into unsettling situations where time bends, death speaks, fate intervenes, or moral reckoning arrives unexpectedly. With its stark black-and-white visuals and Serling's iconic narration, *The Twilight Zone* transforms mortality into a thought experiment, asking viewers not just what happens when life ends but what truly matters before it does.

Many episodes confront death directly, from sudden endings and missed second chances to visions of the afterlife and the fear of oblivion. Others examine symbolic deaths: the death of identity, the death of compassion, or the slow erosion of humanity under fear and power. The series remains remarkably timeless, using speculative storytelling to explore ethical dilemmas, existential anxiety, and the fragile line between control and surrender.

Mortality Themes

- Death as judgment, release, or transformation
- Fear of mortality and fear of meaninglessness
- Afterlife imagined as justice, irony, or mercy
- Legacy and how one is remembered
- Fate versus free will
- The moral consequences of choices made under pressure

Discussion Prompts

1. How does *The Twilight Zone* use fantasy to make conversations about death feel safer or more approachable?

2. Which episodes portray death as punishment, and which portray it as peace or resolution?

3. How does Rod Serling frame mortality as a moral teacher rather than a villain?

4. In what ways do these stories challenge modern ideas about control, technology, and progress?

5. Why do these episodes still resonate decades later?

6. Which episode most changed how you think about death, and why did it resonate with you personally?

Notable Mortality-Focused Episodes

- **"Nothing in the Dark" (Season 3, Episode 16)**

  An elderly woman hides from Death until he arrives as a gentle, compassionate guide.

- **"The Hitch-Hiker" (Season 1, Episode 16)**

  This episode a chilling exploration of denial of one's own death and the inevitability of acceptance.

- **"Time Enough at Last" (Season 1, Episode 8)**

  This one offers a cruelly ironic take on isolation, survival, and the fragility of second chances.

Movie Pairings and Activities

- Pair the series with *It's a Wonderful Life* (1946) to explore alternate realities and life-review themes.

- Or pair it with *Defending Your Life* (1991) for contrasting visions of judgment after death.

- Screen one episode and invite viewers to rewrite the ending from a different moral perspective.

- Ask participants which episode best reflects their own fears or hopes about death.

Final Thought

The Twilight Zone reminds us that death does not always arrive with warning, but meaning is always available. By confronting fear, fate, and finality head-on, the series invites us to live more consciously, more kindly, and with an awareness that the clock is always ticking even when we pretend it is not.

Television Shows and Series: Closing Thoughts

Television teaches us that death rarely arrives neatly wrapped in final words or perfect closure. It happens mid-season, mid-argument, mid-life. And then the story continues, because for the living, it must.

These episodes and series remind us that grief unfolds over time, just like character development. Some losses are processed in a single episode; others ripple through years of storytelling. Humor often shows up alongside heartbreak, not to minimize it but to make it survivable. Again and again, we see that the most meaningful moments surrounding death are not grand speeches but ordinary acts of care, honesty, and connection.

If these shows prompt you to laugh uncomfortably, cry unexpectedly, or rethink how you want to be remembered, they've done their job. Television, at its best, reflects our lives back to us, including the parts we avoid discussing. When it comes to mortality, that reflection can be both sobering and deeply reassuring.

After all, even when the episode ends, the conversation doesn't have to.

THE ".6" IN 98.6 MORTALITY MOVIES: NOTABLE MORTALITY-RELATED SCENES IN FILMS

These films are not quite Mortality Movies, but they contain notable scenes that touch on death, dying, funerals, grief, or the rituals and missteps surrounding them. These moments offer surprisingly rich opportunities for conversation and reflection about how we understand mortality in everyday life. They model mistakes, show some best practices, and can spark discussion, with humor or pathos.

The Big Lebowski **(1998, R, 1 h 57 min):** This cult classic by the Coen brothers is laced with profanity and generally has nothing to do with death until bowling buddy Donny has a coronary outside the bowling alley during a showdown with a group of nihilists. The two scenes that follow are unexpectedly instructive.

The Dude and Walter meet with a funeral director at the mortuary to get their friend's cremated remains. Shocked at the price of an urn for their friend's ashes, Walter asks, "Is there a Ralph's around here?" In this moment, Walter demonstrates how to pursue your options as a funeral consumer. He's asserting his rights provided by the Federal Trade Commission's Funeral Rule, which allows consumers to provide their own casket or urn rather than purchase one from the funeral home. Ralph's is a Southern California grocery store chain. A five-pound Folger's coffee can makes a perfectly serviceable urn.

The next scene, they attempt to scatter Donny's remains from a cliff overlooking the ocean. Walter delivers a rambling eulogy that focuses more on himself than on his friend. When he releases the ashes, the wind blows them directly into the Dude's face. The lesson is practical and memorable. Always know which way the wind is blowing before scattering cremated remains. And remember that a eulogy should honor the deceased, not the speaker.

Bill and Ted's Bogus Journey **(1991, PG, 1 h 33 min):** This sequel sends Bill and Ted into the afterlife, where they parody the iconic chess match from *The Seventh Seal.* In order to return to the land of the living, they challenge the Grim Reaper to a series of games and defeat him at Battleship, Clue, Twister, and others.

Death returns them to life and later joins their band. "Our bass player, the Duke of Spook, the Doc of Shock, the Man with No Tan, please say hello to Death Himself, the Grim Reaper!" Played entirely for laughs, the film portrays Death as approachable, fallible, and oddly cooperative. It is a pop culture example of softening the fear of death through humor, turning an existential threat into a comic companion.

Diamonds Are Forever **(1971, PG, 2 h):** A diamond smuggling investigation leads James Bond to Las Vegas where he visits the Slumber, Inc. funeral home to have his "brother" cremated. Bond takes the urn, ostensibly filled with diamonds, to the Garden of Remembrance Mausoleum and retrieves an envelope of cash.

He is soon knocked unconscious by two henchmen and awakens inside a casket, which is inside a cremation retort. Just moments before incineration, the process is stopped and Bond escapes.

Although wildly unrealistic, the scene provides a rare cinematic look inside a cremation retort. For many viewers, it may be their first visual reference point for cremation equipment. It illustrates how movies often shape expectations about death care more powerfully than real-world experience ever does.

Due Date **(2010, R, 1 h 35 min):** In this comedy, high-strung father-to-be Peter Highman, played by Robert Downey Jr., is forced into a cross-country road trip with aspiring actor Ethan Tremblay, played by Zach Galifianakis, in order to arrive in time for his child's birth. Ethan carries his father's cremated remains in a coffee can.

The remains are mistakenly used to brew a pot of coffee, spilled, gathered up, and eventually scattered in a surprisingly tender moment in the desert Southwest. While it's unlikely most people would confuse cremated remains with coffee grounds, the scene highlight how unfamiliar many people are with what cremated remains actually look like.

***Four Weddings and a Funeral* (1994, R, 1 h 57 min):** As the title promises, this romantic comedy includes a funeral. It's as beautifully produced as each of the weddings and profoundly moving with the recitation of W. H. Auden's poem, *Funeral Blues.* The poem begins with the line, "Stop all the clocks." The moment captures how time can seem to halt for those closest to the deceased, even as the rest of the world continues moving forward. This experience is deeply familiar to anyone in acute grief and gives the film one of its most emotionally resonant scenes.

***Fried Green Tomatoes* (1991, PG-13, 2 h 10 min):** This warm and layered story of female friendship and personal growth includes a quiet death scene that echoes the imagery of *Funeral Blues.* As the death occurs, the clock in the room is stopped, visually reinforcing the idea that grief suspends time. The moment preserves the significance of the loss, as well as the time of death. The stopped clock becomes a simple but powerful metaphor for how grief freezes a moment while the world moves on.

***He Died with a Felafel in His Hand* (2001, Not Rated, 1 h 47 min):** This quirky Australian independent film follows a group of young people sharing a series of communal living spaces. As the title suggests, one of them dies. In one of the film's most memorable scenes, his cremated remains are poured into a fire pit, known in Australian slang as a "barbie." Each housemate places an object of significance into the flames offers a few parting words. The scene beautifully illustrates how informal participant-led rituals can be just as meaningful as traditional funerals, especially for chosen families who create their own structures of care and remembrance.

***Meet the Parents* (2000, PG-13, 1 h 48 min):** This comedy includes a scene that painfully demonstrates the risks of keeping cremated remains at home. During a tense dinner with his future in-laws, Greg Focker, played by Ben Stiller, pops a champagne cork that knocks the ceramic urn holding Grandma's cremated remains, sending it crashing the floor. The family cat then treats the spilled remains like litter. The moment is played for laughs, but it offers a clear practical lesson. Cremated remains deserve a secure and intentional resting place, particularly in households with pets, children, or frequent chaos.

***The Princess Bride* (1987, PG, 1 h 38 min):** This romantic comedy fairy-tale adventure, directed by Rob Reiner, gave us countless memorable lines, including the excellent advice, "Hello. My name is Inigo Montoya. You killed my father. *Prepare to die.*" [My emphasis] There is also a hysterical scene featuring Billy Crystal as Miracle Max, who brings the hero Westley back to life. While entirely fantastical, the film plays with the idea that death is not always final. This theme appears repeatedly across mythology, fairy tales, and modern afterlife narratives, where death can be delayed, reversed, or negotiated under the right conditions.

***Soylent Green* (1973, PG, 1 h 37 min):** Set in the dystopian future of 2022, the world is overheated, overcrowded and depleted of resources. Starvation and despair are widespread, and medical aid in dying is presented as a calm, serene exit option. Edward G. Robinson appears in his final film role as Sol Roth, a man weary of living in a world that is slowly collapsing. When he chooses to die, he is offered music, images of nature, and a serene environment as he takes a potion that peacefully ends his life. This scene stands as one of cinema's earliest portrayals of medical aid in dying, long before the topic entered mainstream public discourse.

***The Truman Show* (1998, PG, 1 h 43 min):** Jim Carrey plays Truman Burbank, an insurance salesman whose entire life is a television reality show, though he is unaware of it. In one poignant scene, Truman speaks on the phone while trying to close a sale and invokes the unpredictability of life and death. "Life is fragile," he says, and he makes the sale. The moment highlights how casually mortality is often referenced in everyday language.

Even when used rhetorically or transactionally, the idea of death still carries emotional weight and quiet power.

***The Vikings* (1958, 1 h 56 min):** This swashbuckling historical drama ends with a visually striking Viking funeral that has had an outsized influence on popular culture. Although historically inaccurate, the scene has profoundly shaped modern assumptions about Viking death rituals. After Kirk Douglas and Tony Curtis swordfight to the death, the victor declares, "Prepare a funeral for a Viking." The body is placed on a boat, pushed out to sea, and set ablaze with flaming arrows. This dramatic image has been idealized as an honorable way to send off the dead and has been repeated in films such as *First Knight* (1995), *Rocket Gibraltar* (1988), *Eulogy* (2004), and *The Living Wake* (2007). This scene demonstrates how cinematic rituals often replace historical reality in the public imagination.

***Zoolander* (2001, R, 1 h 30 min):** This slapstick comedy about male fashion models does not focus heavily on mortality. However, it includes a funeral scene following the senseless deaths of three models in a freak gasoline fight accident. Derek Zoolander's eulogy is a masterclass in narcissism and a near-perfect example of how *not* to speak at a funeral. His reflection afterward, "Oh, I thought you were going to say what a bad eugooglizer I was," neatly underscores the scene's critique of self-centered, performative grief.

These films remind us that death education does not occur only in solemn dramas or documentaries. It also sneaks in through comedy, satire, fantasy or outright absurdity. These brief scenes can linger long after the credits roll, quietly shaping how audiences think about death, funerals, remembrance, and the responsibilities of the living. Sometimes the lesson arrives sideways, wrapped in laughter, and lands when we least expect it.

MORTALITY MOVIE EVENT AND DISCUSSION GUIDE

Talking about death does not have to be heavy, clinical, or intimidating. In fact, some of the most meaningful conversations about mortality begin in the dark, with a bowl of popcorn, a familiar story, and other people who are also quietly paying attention. Mortality Movie events use film as a gentle entry point into discussions many of us avoid until we have no choice.

Whether held in a living room, library, funeral home, or community space, these gatherings create an atmosphere where reflection feels natural, curiosity is welcomed, and no one is put on the spot. This guide offers practical suggestions for hosting a Mortality Movie Night or Matinee that invites connection, conversation, and insight, without requiring anyone to have the "right" words about death.

Hosting a Mortality Movie Night or Mortality Movie Matinee is one of the most accessible ways to invite meaningful conversations about death, grief, and living fully. Movies give people something concrete to respond to, which can lower anxiety and open the door to honest reflection. A daytime matinee option is especially helpful for those who prefer not to drive at night.

This guide will help you plan, host, and facilitate a Mortality Movie event that feels welcoming, thoughtful, and surprisingly enjoyable.

Step 1: Choose the Film or Episode

Select a film or television episode that fits your audience and setting. Consider the group's comfort level with language, sexual content, violence, or emotionally intense material.

Always preview the film yourself. Even movies you have seen before may land differently in a group setting or reveal scenes that are not a good fit for your community. Trust your instincts here. There is no shortage of excellent options in this book.

Step 2: Set the Date, Time, and Location

Choose a date and time that work for your intended audience. Evening events often feel social and cozy. Afternoon matinees can be more accessible for older adults or anyone who avoids nighttime driving.

If the event is held in a public or commercial space such as a funeral home, library, community center, or business location, you will need a public performance license to legally show the film. Licensing can be obtained through services such as the Motion Picture Licensing Corporation (MPLC.org), Swank Motion Pictures (Swank.com), Criterion Pictures USA (CriterionPicUSA.com), or other licensing avenues.

If the event takes place in a private home, a license is not required.

Step 3: Promote the Event

Let people know what you are offering and why it matters. Emphasize conversation, connection, and curiosity rather than education or therapy.

Promotion options include:

- Email lists or newsletters
- Social media posts and event pages
- Meetup groups
- Eventbrite and other online calendar listings
- Postcards or flyers
- Word of mouth

Be clear about the film, the date and time, and what participants can expect. Reassure people that they do not need special knowledge or personal experience with loss to attend.

Step 4: Create a Comfortable Atmosphere

Food and drink help people relax and signal that this is a shared experience, not a lecture.

Simple movie snacks work well:

- Popcorn (offer different flavorings to customize)
- Chocolate or candy
- Cookies
- Water, coffee, tea, or soft drinks

Decorating with Movie Night touches can add warmth without turning the event into a theme party. Signage, napkins, cups, and plates from party supply stores are more than sufficient.

Step 5: Welcome and Set the Tone

Begin by welcoming participants and briefly explaining the Mortality Movie concept.

You may wish to share that this approach grew out of Gail Rubin's experience hosting Death Cafes in Albuquerque, New Mexico. When she added film viewing events to the mix for death discussion, more men and new people began participating. Movies give people a great place to start the conversation.

Invite participants to introduce themselves and share what drew them to the event. This step helps people feel seen and often deepens the discussion later. If the group is larger than about 30 people, you may choose to skip introductions to save time.

When introducing the film, use information from this book to highlight key mortality themes to watch for. Keep it brief. You are opening a door, not delivering a summary.

Step 6: During the Screening

In smaller or more intimate settings, it is perfectly fine for participants and the facilitator to make occasional comments during the film. This can feel playful and communal, much like the comedy television show *Mystery Science Theater 3000*.

If your group prefers quiet viewing, set that expectation up front. Either approach is valid. The goal is engagement, not reverence.

Step 7: Let the Credits Roll

After the film ends, allow the credits to play in full. Many movies include additional scenes, humor, or emotional resolution during the credits.

If people begin talking before the credits finish, turn the volume down and let the film continue to run. If something noteworthy appears, simply turn the sound back up.

This small pause gives people time to breathe before jumping into discussion.

Step 8: Guide the Conversation

Begin by inviting open reactions. Ask something simple such as, "What stood out to you?" or "What are you still thinking about?"

From there, you can move among the discussion prompts provided in the book. There is no need to follow them in order. Let the conversation flow naturally.

A few facilitation tips:

- Silence is not a failure. A quiet moment often invites deeper sharing.
- You do not need to respond to every comment. Let participants respond to each other.
- Gently redirect if one person dominates the conversation.
- Normalize differing reactions. There is no single "right" response to a film.

Your role is to hold the space, not to provide answers.

Step 9: Closing the Event

As you wrap up, consider inviting participants to reflect on possible actions inspired by the film, such as:

- Planning final disposition wishes
- Completing advance medical directives
- Recognizing that grief is a journey, not a problem to solve

- Resolving to live more fully and intentionally

- Talking with loved ones about what matters

You can also remind attendees that they can continue exploring these themes by watching more films from *98.6 Mortality Movies to See Before You Die.*

If you have another event planned, announce it. Then thank everyone sincerely for showing up and engaging.

Step 10: Follow-Up

For end-of-life businesses such as funeral homes, hospices, insurance organizations, or financial planners, follow up with attendees after the event. Make sure you have collected contact information, and send a brief thank-you message with details about future events or resources.

A Final Word

Congratulations. You have just hosted a Mortality Movie Night or Matinee.

You created space for conversation, reflection, and connection around topics many people avoid. That is no small thing. Movies may roll credits and fade to black, but the conversations they spark often linger, quietly changing how people think about death and, more importantly, how they live.

ABOUT THE AUTHOR

Gail Rubin, CT, widely known as *The Doyenne of Death®*, is a nationally recognized death educator, speaker, author, and film curator who has made it her life's work to help people talk about the one thing they're most likely to avoid: death. With warmth, wit, and a deep respect for human stories, Gail uses humor, popular culture, and movies to transform uncomfortable end-of-life conversations into meaningful, even enjoyable, discussions.

She is the award-winning author of *A Good Goodbye: Funeral Planning for Those Who Don't Plan to Die, Kicking the Bucket List: 100 Downsizing and Organizing Things to Do Before You Die, Hail and Farewell: Cremation Ceremonies, Templates and Tips, The Before I Die Festival in a Box*, and *98.6 Mortality Movies to See Before You Die*. Her books blend practical guidance with compassion, empowering readers to plan ahead, reduce stress on loved ones, and live more intentionally, because contemplating mortality tends to sharpen one's appreciation for life.

Gail is the coordinator of the award-winning Before I Die New Mexico Festival, an annual community event that brings together professionals and the public to explore death-related topics through workshops, conversations, art, and education. She is also a pioneer of the Death Cafe movement in the United States, helping normalize open, judgment-free conversations about death long before it became a cultural trend. She also created the Newly-Dead® Game, which tests couples on how well they know each other's last wishes.

A certified thanatologist (CT), Gail is trained in death, grief, and bereavement education and is known for her engaging speaking style that combines expert knowledge with humor and humanity. She frequently uses films as conversation starters, hosting the Mortality Movies TV series and Mortality Movie Night events where audiences explore themes of mortality, loss, and legacy, often laughing, sometimes crying, and always thinking a little deeper by the end.

Her ideas have reached a global audience through TEDx talks, including her 2015 TEDx presentation on the importance of starting end-of-life conversations *before* a death occurs and her 2025 TEDxABQ talk addressing medical aid in dying. In recognition of her leadership and impact, *Albuquerque Business First* named her one of their Women of Influence in 2019.

Gail's professional affiliations include the Association for Death Education and Counseling, which honored her with the 2024 Community Educator Award, as well as the International Cemetery, Cremation and Funeral Association, Toastmasters International, and the National Speakers Association.

Her personal mission is summed up in her signature motto: "Talking about sex won't make you pregnant. Talking about funerals won't make you dead."

Through her writing, speaking, films, and festivals, Gail Rubin continues to help people face mortality with curiosity, courage, and a sense of humor, one conversation (and one movie) at a time. Learn more at www.AGoodGoodbye.com.

9 780984 596287